Father of California Wine:
Agoston Haraszthy

Father of California Wine:
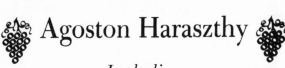
Agoston Haraszthy

Including

GRAPE CULTURE, WINES & WINE-MAKING

Edited by THEODORE SCHOENMAN

Foreword by Robert L. Balzer

CAPRA PRESS
Santa Barbara - 1979

Jacket design by Marcia Burtt.
Production by Don French and Mary Schlesinger.
Printed and bound by R.R. Donnelley & Sons.

Library of Congress Cataloging in Publication Data

Haraszthy, Agoston, 1812-1869.
    Father of California wine.

    Reprint of the 1862 ed. published by Harper &
Brothers, New York, under title: Grape culture,
wines, and winemaking.
    1. Viticulture—Europe. 2. Wine and wine
making—Europe. 3. Viticulture—California.
4. Wind and wine making—California. I. Schoenman, Theodore.
II. Title.
SB391.H25 1979   641.2′2′094   79-200
ISBN 0-88496-092-7

CAPRA PRESS
P.O. Box 2068
Santa Barbara, California 93120

For Ilonka

AUTHOR'S NOTE

This book like all of my work, was written in collaboration with my wife Helen Benedek Schoenman, with whom I work, study and share so many experiences. Our discussions about Haraszthy and other political refugees have continued over several years and our ideas have been so intertwined that this book would be incomplete and could not have come into being without her contribution.

My special thanks are due to Corlice Wendling of the Santa Barbara Public Library for her valuable research assistance.

The original illustrations are by courtesy of The Wine Institute, San Francisco and the Buena Vista Winery, Sonoma.

—T.S.

FOREWORD

ROBERT LAWRENCE BALZER

Among the treasures of my library is a calf-bound volume, bearing on its spine, in gold lettering on the black panel, GRAPE CULTURE, WINES, AND WINE-MAKING. One must turn to the title page to discover that the author was A. Haraszthy, that this first edition was published by Harper & Brothers of Franklin Square, in New York, in 1862. I have read and re-read it countless times. It has been the source of inspiration for not only dozens of essays which I have written on California wines, but there are as many vignettes which I have read aloud to my classes in wine appreciation. These always include the letter given to Agoston Haraszthy by President Lincoln's Secretary of State, William H. Seward on the 6th of July 1861. These were Civil War times, but Haraszthy, the first true-believer in California wines embarked upon the most significant mission of agricultural purpose, certainly in California's history, and possibly in the annals of American agriculture. It is from these "100,000 vines, embracing about 1400 varieties" that today's multi-million dollar California wine industry was born. The saga of those vines, bought in all the varied *climats* of Europe's wine-lands, becomes an unending saga of viticulture. It remains replete with both mystery and awe. To know the full story of those bundles of vine cuttings, where and how they found their way into California soil, is only a small part of this veritable *roman à clef*. There is no chapter without adventure and drama. The protagonist, as story-teller, is irresistible. To know, beforehand, his tragic fate gives the whole volume the cast of heroic tragedy. But all along the way there is the buoyancy of Haraszthy's indefatigable energy and unbounded enthusiasm.

That this work of Haraszthy is being made available to the American reading public today, who, by the hundreds of thousands, even millions, are staunch advocates of California wines, is a boon. It enriches the pleasure of pouring these wines, of savoring their bouquet drawn from not only all the wine valleys, but the hillsides. It was this intrepid Hungarian who was the first in America to take vines to the hills for non-irrigated planting.

We are also indebted to the devotion of Theodore Schoenman for researching the life of Agoston Haraszthy as only a fellow countryman might. His work was not stopped by language barriers. But beyond these limitations which would have penalized the work of a more ordinary layman, is the cultural bloodline with the inherent understanding of this bold figure, so arresting upon first meeting, titles were thrust upon him by the majesty of his bearing. It really matters not a whit whether he was baron, count, or colonel. The man is here in his work. His legacy is everywhere on the winelands of California, greening the landscape, and heady with scent in every vintage. Buena Vista Vineyards and Buena Vista Winery are not only alive and thriving today in Sonoma County, but should be the first objective in the California visitors' wine pilgrimage.

Once upon a time, in the cellar caves of Buena Vista in Sonoma, when Antonia and Frank Bartholomew had brought the restoration of the Haraszthy estate to a condition of sufficiently prideful beauty for guests to behold, I was invited along with perhaps another two dozen friends. General "Hap" Arnold was there. Together, we all walked the pathway across the sloping meadow down to the eucalyptus-lined creek, and into the winery. The neat and precise line-up of golden oak ovals made an aisle to the barrel-lined caves dug into the hillside. It was late afternoon in autumn. The sun had set. The glow in the winery came from candles set upon the ledge of every cask and barrel. The effect was more than stunning. It was eery.... One hundred years before, at the Convent of Eberbach of the Rhineland, Agoston Haraszthy had been just so honored with a candlelight reception in the cellar. The grandeur of the moment is a part of the story that follows.

Shakespeare put this taunting rebuke into the mouth of one of his characters. . ."What the great will do, the lesser will prattle of." Haraszthy has had his detractors, and it is our fondest hope that with this published work, all the quibbling thrusts and parries will be dissolved. They were made by those of limited vision who could not comprehend the magnitude of this man and his driving promotional genius. We are where we are today in the California wine industry by Haraszthy's ambitious drive and almost vision-ary goals. It is a privilege to be able to acknowledge this debt in printed words.

ROBERT LAWRENCE BALZER
Santa Ana, California
December 30, 1978

FATHER OF CALIFORNIA WINE:

Agoston Haraszthy

The Gold Rush years produced those legendary figures of California history: Leland Stanford, Mark Hopkins, C.P. Huntington, Charles Crocker—the big four of the central Pacific Railroad—as well as Jim Fair, Jim Flood, Lucky Baldwin, George Hearst, and Billy Ralston of the Mother Lode and Comstock Lode fame. Each amassed a vast fortune and exerted enormous influence on the social, economic, and political development of the Golden State. Yet today, Sutter's gold and Comstock Lode silver fade into insignificance compared to the impact and value of the huge wine and grape industry. And when speaking of wine and grapes, the name of Agoston Haraszthy is indelibly inscribed on the pages of California history. Although this "Johnny Appleseed" of grapes did not accumulate wealth or political influence in his lifetime, one hundred years after his death a grateful Congress honored him in a joint resolution and officially acknowledged him "Father of California's Viticulture." No unsung pioneer contributed more to the future prosperity of his adopted country and none is more deserving of rescue from a century of unmerited neglect. His legacy, in 1976, was over one-half million acres planted in grapes and over 500 million gallons of wine. The recognition of his services was long overdue.

Heraldic records indicate that the Haraszthys belonged to the ancient nobility of Hungary. They were continually involved in the historic struggles against the conquering Turks and the oppressive rule of the Hapsburgs. Yet, the family's fame and fortune were not gained on the battlefields of Hungary but in its orchards and vineyards: cultivation of fruits and prime grapes was a family tradition, and they had pioneered the cultivation of silkworms as well. The development of improved vines and the making of fine wines were essential parts of Agoston Haraszthy's heritage.

Unfortunately only the sketchiest documentation exists about his childhood, adolescence, and young manhood. Most of the data cited in the family chronicle are unverifiable, but existing records confirm that Haraszthy was born on August 30, 1812, at Futak on the family estate in the province of Bácska. He was the only son of Charles Haraszthy de Mokcsa (later in America known as General Haraszthy) and his wife Anna, nee Halász. He was probably their only child as there is no record or mention of brothers or sisters.

As was customary with Hungarian nobles, Haraszthy received a traditional education in the classics, Greek and Latin, and went on to study law. He also had a thorough training in public adminis- tration and the management of the family estate. At eighteen he became an officer in the Royal Hungarian bodyguard of Francis I, first Emperor of Austria-Hungary, nephew of Marie Antoinette and Napoleon's father-in-law. The select corps was composed of the youth of the top level of Hungarian aristocracy. Many young officers of the guard learned several foreign languages and de- veloped scholarly and literary interests. Others turned to eco- nomic and/or political studies. They were among the first in Hungary who familiarized themselves with the progressive ideas of the West and the liberal principles of the young American democracy. Many of them became the advocates and leaders of Hungary's Age of Reform in the first part of the nineteenth century.

From his service in the Guard young Haraszthy returned to his native county and assumed his hereditary office of honorary Lord Lieutenant. Ex-officio he was a delegate of his county to the Diet in Pozsony where he quickly formed close associations and friendships with Baron Wesselényi (a brilliant and daring Tran- sylvanian leader of the radical reformists) and with the spellbind- ing firebrand, Louis Kossuth.

In 1831 the Polish revolution was crushed and many unfortu- nate Poles driven from their country sought refuge in Hungary. Among them was the noble family of Dedinsky. Haraszthy fell in love with their daughter Eleonora. They were married in 1834 and in the following year their first son was born. He was named Géza after a mythological Hungarian chieftain. Géza was destined to become a cited and decorated hero of the American Civil War. Although nothing in the official archives confirms it, the family chronicle asserts that in 1835 Haraszthy became the private secretary of the Regent of Hungary, the Archduke Joseph. Then, when in 1837 Wesselényi and Kossuth were arrested and charged with treason, Haraszthy retired to his estate and acted as county magistrate. He may have felt himself a marked man for in March of 1840 he embarked on a journey through Europe and England. Accompanied by his eighteen year old cousin Charles Halász he sailed on the packetboat "Samson" and after a tedious passage of forty-two days landed in New York in June 1840. Haraszthy in his book *Travels in North America* (1844) makes no mention of any political motivation for his flight, although later in Wisconsin he often spoke of being forced to flee political persecution.

In New York he was received with great fanfare by two Americans, Messrs. Whitlock and Hislip who had been guests at his estate at Futak the previous year. His hosts also included Hamilton Jackson, the brother of former President Andrew Jackson. He was wined and dined and entertained in high style during his brief stay in New York, but he was anxious to push on, to see as much of "this fabulous continent" as possible. His friends gave him a boisterous farewell party at the luxurious Hotel Clinton, and armed with many letters of recommendation, he set out on an odyssey of two years. He travelled up the Hudson Valley and through the Erie Canal to the Great Lakes. He grew ecstatic when confronted with the natural wonder of Niagara Falls. He stopped and described most of the fast growing cities of the continent, all the while making detailed notes of his observations on the economic and social conditions. His book is crammed with statistical tables of all imaginable commercial, legal, political, even meteorological data.

When in Washington, he was received with great courtesy by President Tyler who expressed lively interest in Haraszthy's plans for the establishment of commercial relations between Hungary and the U.S. Daniel Webster, Henry Clay, Lewis Cass, and other notables were his sponsors. With amusement Haraszthy relates his reception: "I had many onlookers stare at me when I presented myself to the President in my full Hungarian Guard dress uniform. Everyone admired my heavily gold braided and richly trimmed dolman, but they could not understand why one should wear two jackets at the same time, nor could they see the purpose of the belt. They all agreed though that there is no more splendid and glamorous uniform than the Hungarian. A few days later I was invited to a presidential soirée. I was informed by friends that the President would like me to wear my dress uniform because the many ladies invited would be curious to see it. I complied with the request but I felt uncomfortable all evening, noticing that all eyes were riveted on me."[1]

Pushing deep into the unknown wilderness of the West he crisscrossed the state of Illinois and the territories of Wisconsin, Iowa, and Kansas. Accompanied by Lord Malgred, an Englishman, and a Dr. Rogers, his traveling companion on the "Samson," he spent fifteen weeks among the tribes of the Prairie Indians, especially the Sac and Fox. He joined them in their hunting and fishing expeditions. He studied their customs, their lifestyle, their social organization, all of which he described in fascinating detail in his book.

Increasingly he became captivated by the natural beauty of the virgin continent and was overwhelmed by the immense potential of its unexploited natural resources.

To a man of Haraszthy's fertile imagination and humanist sympathies, the new untamed country, the fertile prairie overlooked by gentle, wooded hills with the mighty Wisconsin River flowing by, brought visions of thousands of Europe's land hungry peasants cultivating the rich soil and creating a hopeful future for themselves and their families. He wrote: "My God—I thought —how many people are in utter misery in Europe, unable to provide their meagre needs whereas here nature offers just for the taking millions of acres of rich black soil which just needs to be turned over to produce a bountiful harvest...."[2]

Ever the man of action Haraszthy quickly translated his admiration for America into deeds. His appreciative eye recognized the potential of the land, and he bought a small parcel on the Wisconsin River front from one of the earliest settlers and shortly after, in partnership with Robert Bryant, an Englishman and recent immigrant, bought 10,000 acres for $1.25 an acre from the government. The partnership covered a wide range of enterprise, but the building of a town was the principal aim. Bryant had full confidence in Haraszthy's grandiose plans for development, in his scheme of promoting large scale immigration, in his elaborate design of land sales to farmers, and in the subdivision of the projected townsite into building lots. His humanitarian instincts, however, did not preclude a highly profitable venture for himself and his partner.

"Originally I came to America for one reason, namely to see this blessed land for myself. The thought of acquiring property and settling here, never crossed my mind. I must admit that I had hopes to establish commercial relations between my homeland and North America,"[3] he had written in his diary. But his family, his wife, his three sons, Géza, Attila and Árpád, all named after legendary princes of Hungarian mythology, were still in Hungary and he was persona non grata with the Austrian authorities. Through the intervention of General Lewis Cass he was guaranteed safe-conduct and permission to stay one year. In early 1842 he rejoined his family but did not stay long for he persuaded his father to liquidate the ancestral estate and to join him with the entire family in the venture in the New World. By selling his own lands and his wife's dowry he managed to amass a very substantial capital to carry out his promotional plans.

Before his return to America in the fall of 1842 Haraszthy arranged in Pest for the publication of his *Travels in North America* which appeared in 1844. The book had a significant impact and was extensively reviewed in leading journals and periodicals. Haraszthy's portrait of America and the phenomenal opportunities available on the western frontier triggered the immigration of thousands of Hungarian, Austrian, Czech, Polish, and Swiss peasants and artisans. Entranced by Haraszthy's lyric description of Wisconsin, many of them settled there.

Returning to his primitive settlement which he named romantically "Széptáj" (Beautiful View) he plunged into hectic activity. Our town builder first constructed roads, built bridges, operated a sawmill, a gristmill, and a brickyard. To supply the growing population he opened a general store and imported not only the necessities of life but luxury items as well. Aside from his various commercial and industrial ventures he experimented with several branches of agriculture. His cultivation of grapes however proved to be a failure. The unsuitable terrain and climate defeated his best efforts. He scored a very significant first, however, by successfully growing hops, and his hopyard produced a two million dollar crop within a decade. He also planted wheat and corn on a large enough scale to contract with the government to supply Fort Winnebago with grain. His extensive operation in animal husbandry was another first in Wisconsin. He introduced sheep raising in the Territory and at one time owned a herd of nearly 2000 head.

The location of Széptáj on the Wisconsin River soon focused his attention on the transportation opportunities offered by the waterway. He began with the operation of the first ferryboat across the Wisconsin. Later, foreseeing the great potential of service down the Wisconsin and Mississippi all the way to St. Louis and to the great port of New Orleans, he bought a steamboat in Pittsburgh on which the original buyer had defaulted and put it in service hauling passengers and freight between Fort Winnebago and Galena, Illinois, the great lead mining center. Haraszthy's packet the "Rock River" which steamed as far as St. Paul on the Upper Mississippi was well known in Wisconsin Territory.

Haraszthy's educational background, his experience in public administration, and his unmistakable promotional genius inevitably marked him for leadership. He organized and headed the first Emigrant Association of Wisconsin to assist the stream of settlers who were persuaded by the large number of flamboyant pamphlets and extravagant advertisements to undertake the arduous trek to Wisconsin. Although Haraszthy prospered by selling them land and supplies, he was keenly conscious of his responsibility for their welfare. He founded the Humamanist Society in 1842 which made Sauk City (the ultimate name of Széptáj) known all over Europe as the "Freethinkers Heaven" and attracted such nationally known speakers as Robert Ingersoll, Carl Schurz, and Franz Siegel.

Tales about Haraszthy still told in Wisconsin, where he was known as Count Haraszthy, are almost heroic in character.

"He was an arresting figure: a large active man, very dark with black hair, wide black mustache and full black beard. His dark eyes reflected the moods of a dreamer and a doer. He loved to ride hard and hunt game. His prowess as a hunter was legendary. Wearing a green silk hunting shirt with a wide silken sash of flaming red he was seen many times riding through brush and bramble, laughing while the

thorns tore at his expensive dress. As his town rose from the mud of the prairie, he always moved about wearing a stovepipe hat and carrying a cane, giving orders in several languages to foreign born workmen. He seemed born to command, yet his friends found him generous to a fault. He was of a poetic disposition and was a brilliant conversationalist. He loved to entertain at lavish parties and was greatly admired as the perfect host. His likable eccentricities were still talked about at the turn of the century."[4]

With all his diverse ventures Haraszthy had made a great deal of money, yet by the spring of 1848 he found himself in difficulties. His holdings were heavily mortgaged and his creditors were pressing. His famed generosity in helping his neighbors, the free hand with which he extended credit, and, above all, his inability to collect the debts owed him, led to his financial undoing. This was probably the principal reason for his decision to pull up stakes and get a fresh start in the West. Contributing factors may have been his father's gout, his own chronic asthma, and the invitingly warm climate of California. Then again it may have been his never-abandoned vision of successfully growing grapes and making fine wines which had been a dismal failure in Wisconsin.

In 1848 Wisconsin attained statehood, and Haraszthy's spectacular exploits in his eight years there had contributed much to it. Not unmindful of his services, the legislature honored him with a public dinner in the capital before his departure.

The village of Széptáj was renamed Haraszthyville within a few years, but when the German population had difficulty pronouncing it, the town was renamed Westfield and eventually Sauk City. Haraszthy's pioneering activities in territorial Wisconsin are romanticized in several historical novels. The best known are *Restless is the River* by August Derleth and *A House Too Old* by Mark Schorer, both authors native of Sauk City.[5]

On Christmas day 1848, Haraszthy, his wife, their six children, Géza, Attila, Árpád and the three born in America, Béla, Ida, and Ottilia, together with his father and stepmother, drove in two sleighs to Madison where they made all the preparations for the overland journey to California. A caravan of considerable size started out in the early spring of 1849. It included Thomas W. Sutherland, at one time U.S. Attorney for the Wisconsin Territory, whose mother had married Haraszthy's father in 1848 three years after the death of Haraszthy's mother.

There is only a sketchy record about the trek to California. They left St. Joseph, Missouri in the early summer of 1849 and struck out along the Santa Fe Trail. Haraszthy was elected captain and master of the train which consisted of twenty wagons. The party crossed over the wilderness of Kansas, Texas, New Mexico, and Arizona encountering the usual hardships and fighting off hostile Indian tribes.

Late December 1849 found the wagon train on the border of California. For reasons not quite clear, Haraszthy and family, the Sutherlands, and a few others parted from the larger group which was heading north for the Mother Lode country. Haraszthy's lack of interest in digging for gold was possibly due to his yearning for the warmth of southern California. When the small party of '49ers drove into Warners Hot Springs, the site of the famed Warner Ranch, the owner, Colonel Jonathan T. Warner, son-in-law of Don Pio Pico, the ex-governor of California, was most impressed by the courtly manners and innate elegance of the entire family. He supplied Haraszthy with information about farming and the politics of the area. Haraszthy wasted no time: after appraising his prospects in San Diego which at the time was a frontier village with a population of about 650 (farmers and a few tradesmen, but mostly vaqueros and waterfront idlers) and with the help of his sons Attila and Árpád, he planted a large fruit orchard at San Luis Rey Mission, thirty miles north of San Diego. He studied soil conditions and learned much about the flora and suitable cultivation in the arid climate of the region. Here he learned at first hand from the Mission fathers about the Mission grape which he was surprised to find was of true European origin, a Vitis vinifera. It had been originally brought into Mexico from Spain as early as 1524 while Cortez was governor, and was first planted in San Diego around 1770 by the Mission padres. Although the vine is vigorous and bears well, the fruit makes a poor quality wine. Haraszthy quickly noted its defects and became convinced that plantings of nobler varieties could be commercially viable. He sensed that by planting vines brought directly from Europe he could realize his old dream of producing wine of a quality that could compete with good Hungarian and other European wines. It was here in San Diego that he first began to preach that "good wine can only be made from good grapes."

To put his theory into practice, he and some of his friends bought a tract of 160 acres in Mission Valley, a few miles northeast of San Diego where he planted peach and cherry trees sent from New York and, in February 1851, set out roots and cuttings of grapevines which he had ordered from Europe. But he was dissatisfied with the results. The sub-tropical climate which is so much warmer than that of the traditional wine producing regions, frustrated him. He often complained that because of the lack of winter, his vines did not get their needed rest.

In the meantime his customary method of diversifying his interests found fertile soil in San Diego. In partnership with Don Juan Bandini, a prominent patrician, he organized a livery stable and an omnibus line. He also opened a very profitable butcher shop and at the same time engaged in extensive land speculation. Backed by his associates he subdivided a new development called Middletown where a Haraszthy Street was still in existence until about 1960, and he did not neglect his natural bent for politics. When in March 1850 the county of San Diego was first chartered and the first county election held, his eloquent oratory insured his election to the office of sheriff. Two months later he was chosen the first marshal of the newly incorporated city of San Diego. His father campaigned on his own account and was elected magistrate and land commissioner, while Tom Sutherland became the city attorney.

Haraszthy was a very effective enforcer of the law. In short order he cleaned out what was a tough waterfront town. He was much criticized, however, for his harsh action against neighboring Indian farmers who vehemently protested the intrusion of white ranchers on their ancestral lands and refused to pay the taxes Haraszthy levied on their cattle. His militancy aroused a swarm of anti-Haraszthy sentiment, but he was supported when he beat down the Indian uprising led by Antonio Garra who was hanged for his part. By that time, however, Haraszthy had resigned his posts of sheriff and city marshal, for he had been elected four months earlier as the first representative of the district in the state assembly. He left for Vallejo where the legislature convened before it ultimately moved to Sacramento, the new state capital.

During their short stay in San Diego, the Haraszthys, father and son, seemed to have dominated the town, but they had also been in the center of a curious controversy. They were sharply upbraided in the local press for some peculiar machinations in connection with the building of the first jail in San Diego. The jail story still produces chuckles in San Diego. Even for a frontier town, free gunplay in 1850-51 was phenomenal. With the large number of wild characters floating in and out on their way to the goldfields, a good jail was badly needed. Haraszthy bid for the job and was awarded the contract by the city council headed by his father even though his bid of $5000 was more than double the lowest bid. This raised quite a few eyebrows. Because good quality cement was hard to get, Haraszthy had to use huge cobblestones held together with a mortar of local origin. This was loosened by heavy rains, and when the first prisoner, a harmless drunk, was locked up and a public celebration with a parade and music was held, the prisoner crashed through the wall and calmly sauntered over to the nearest saloon to the immense amusement of the crowd. But Haraszthy not only weathered the storm, in the end he was awarded an additional $2000 to make the jail more secure.

He made his mark in the legislature as well. He successfully lobbied for the expansion of San Diego harbor and for a hospital to care for sick immigrants. He also fought off a determined attempt to create a telegraph monopoly in San Francisco. But his historic proposal to divide California into two states died in the senate. In an eloquent speech he pointed out the iniquity of the high taxes levied on the agricultural south but used for the benefit of the north which was already greatly enriched by the gold strike. On different grounds the idea is still debated today.

His first trip to the north to attend the legislature proved to be the turning point in his career. In mid-session he traveled up and down the state making careful notes on cattle ranches and fruit orchards and keeping a sharp lookout for suitable locations for grapes. Very much aware of the climatic reasons for the failure of his vines in San Diego, he thoroughly explored the Bay area of San Francisco and on an impulsive decision bought a plot of fifty acres near San Francisco's Mission Dolores in March 1852. A few days later he added 160 more acres. At the end of the legislative session he liquidated his holdings in San Diego and except for occasional business visits, never returned.

At his new ranch Haraszthy designed and laid out a nursery and a horticultural garden which he named poetically "Los Flores." With the help of Attila he planted fruit trees and shrubs imported from the East. It was at this time that he received a shipment of six choice rooted vines and 160 cuttings from Hungary. According to the memoirs of Árpád, his mother and the four younger children were in New York and New Jersey where Haraszthy had sent them to get the kind of schooling not obtainable in California. They took up residence in Plainfield, N.J. where they were the neighbors of General Lázár Mészáros, the Minister of War in the Kossuth cabinet and an old comrade of Haraszthy. It was Mészáros who sent Haraszthy the bale of vine cuttings, some of which had originated in Hungary. In the shipment were two small bundles. One was the Muscat of Alexandria and the other was said to be the famous mystery grape, the Zinfandel. The family story claims that the inscription on the vine was so faded that peering through a lens, Haraszthy could hardly decipher "Zinfandel," a name unfamiliar to him. Scores of articles and opinions by experts about the origin and identity of Zinfandel have been written. Many credit Haraszthy with its introduction to California, but others assert that the grape was brought here from New England by one of the several other pioneer growers. However, Haraszthy's role in the development and popularization of its culture was great, and today the Zinfandel is the most widely planted red wine grape in California. Its monetary value and enjoyment during the last 100 years would be hard to measure.

The Muscat of Alexandria which General Mészáros had ordered from Malaga was also of importance, for its introduction founded California's major raisin growing industry. In the view of Maynard Amerine, dean of California oenologists, "The introduction of the Muscat of Alexandria and the Zinfandel constitutes Haraszthy's first important contribution to California viticulture."

While developing "Los Flores" Haraszthy invested heavily in fresh grapes. He bought large quantities around Los Angeles at a fraction of the price commanded in San Francisco where the gold-seeking immigrants were willing to pay high prices.

Haraszthy traveled all over the south of the state buying up the entire output of small vineyards. On his buying expeditions he made detailed notes on the climatic and soil conditions of most vineyards and developed very definite ideas about ways to improve the quality of their product and operation. It was not long before he concluded that because of its cool, foggy summers Mission Dolores and San Francisco were not favorable locations for a vineyard. He was also persuaded that it was essential to import not just a few but many varieties of European vines. By this time he knew that California was blessed with all the ingredients needed to produce the finest quality grapes and wine capable of competing with the best of Europe. In 1853 he started to sell off "Los Flores," and having acquired a large tract at Crystal Springs in San Mateo County, assisted by his sons, he planted thirty acres of his Hungarian grape varieties and the Muscat vines moved from "Los Flores." They also transplanted 20,000 choice fruit trees and raised a large herd of livestock.

It was shortly after his acquisition of Crystal Springs that he became involved in another of his ventures which brought him many anxious moments. Both Haraszthy and his father were enthusiastic experimenters in metallurgy and, according to John Xántus, the naturalist, compatriot, and contemporary, Haraszthy invented a highly efficient gold refining process which he later patented. However, its record is missing from the files of the U.S. Patent Office.

The discovery of gold had attracted several highly trained Hungarian metallurgists to San Francisco with whom Haraszthy formed a partnership in the Eureka Gold and Silver Refining Co., an up to date operation equipped with specially designed machinery. When the San Francisco Mint, which opened in April 1854, was unable to handle the huge volume of gold rolling in from the goldfields, the U.S. Treasury decided to contract private refiners to handle the steadily accumulating backlog. No one was better equipped for this than Haraszthy and his Eureka Refinery and they were given a contract. Although he was appointed assayer of the mint in 1855, the obvious conflict of interest was overlooked because of Haraszthy's reputation for integrity and the government's urgent need. Politics were involved as well: both President Franklin Pierce and M. S. Latham, a leading California congressman, knew that Haraszthy was a prominent and highly esteemed Jeffersonian Democrat.

There was great pressure on the San Francisco Mint for the production of a large volume of coins. From 1855 to 1857 when Haraszthy served as assayer, melter, and refiner, more than $100,000,000 in gold was processed at the mint. But toward the end of 1856, he became worried: the furnaces had to run day and night and, in the absence of charcoal, blowers were used to force a proper draft. This allowed gold particles to escape up the chimney and Haraszthy feared the permissible waste limit may have been exceeded.

J. Ross Browne, the widely read humorist, also had an enviable reputation as an incorruptible treasury agent and was assigned to investigate the mint's performance. Browne's investigation estimated a wastage of $130,000 worth of gold and he suspected additional shortages. In June 1857 Haraszthy resigned his position at the mint and asked for an audit of its accounts. Shortly thereafter Browne presented his case to the U.S. Grand Jury charging Haraszthy with fraud and the Grand Jury indicted him with embezzlement for exceeding the legal limit of waste by $151,000. Browne recommended denial of bail unless Haraszthy turned over all his property in trust to the Treasury in case judgement was rendered against him.

Haraszthy, outraged but also deeply concerned, complied. He sold his interest in the Eureka Refinery and took mortgages on the Crystal Springs ranch and several other tracts. These he deeded to the Treasury in lieu of bond. A storm broke over the affair, and Haraszthy became the central figure of a "cause célèbre." His name was daily in the headlines. His political opponents and many who resented his bold innovations made the most of it. He was denounced as a reckless experimenter and a shady operator, but his defenders praised him as a man of vision and courage.

The resolution of this sensational case was not to come for four years. There were long, monotonous hearings, appeals, and retrials until it was conclusively proven that Haraszthy's original contention was correct. Soot and grime scraped from roofs adjacent to the mint were sent for analysis to the federal mint in Philadelphia where they were found to contain an extraordinarily high percentage of gold. In November 1860, on motion by the U.S. Attorney, the circuit court dismissed the indictment and in March 1861 the jury in a civil suit found "...no evidence in this case to prove the slightest fraud by the defendant."[6]

Haraszthy was exonerated, but the long litigation had been very costly. Suspicion hung over his head and the press kept hinting about ill gotten gains.

During the years spent at the mint and at the Eureka Refinery, Haraszthy continued his experiments with foreign vine varieties at Crystal Springs. All his spare time was devoted to a search for the alchemy of sun, soil, and rain best suited for their growth, and in 1857 his attention was called to the vineyard of General Mariano Guadalupe Vallejo at Sonoma. He had met Vallejo in 1852 at the session of the legislature held in the city named after the General. The names of Vallejo and Sonoma recall an historic moment in northern California. In June 1846, a handful of American settlers, with the concurrence of Captain John Charles Frémont, tried to establish an independent state. On the fourteenth they captured Sonoma and its founder General Vallejo. Then they raised their "Bear Flag" and proclaimed Sonoma the capital of the California Republic. However, in early July they learned that the United States was at war with Mexico and the rebels, abandoning their own plans, joined forces with their fellow Americans to ultimately defeat the Mexicans. Although Sonoma was the capital of California for only twenty-six days, those days are proudly remembered by its citizens who still celebrate on June 14.

General Vallejo, a shrewd politician, quickly and smoothly adjusted to the new rulers and continued to have considerable influence. He was a successful land speculator who had accumulated large holdings in Sonoma County and, with his brother Salvadore, had begun planting grapes as early as 1834. At the time Haraszthy made his first appearance at Sonoma in 1857, Vallejo was the leading vintner. Yet, in the Valley of the Moon, an area about eleven miles long and three miles wide, there were barely fifty acres planted in grapes, all of them the low quality Mission variety.

Vallejo, well aware of Haraszthy's interest in wine, invited him to his estate, Lachrima Montis (Tear of the Mountain), to taste the wine of which he was inordinately proud. Haraszthy eagerly accepted the invitation. With his first glimpse of Sonoma Valley he sensed instantly that his long search had ended. Here was a valley of rich soil, bathed in warm sun, its rolling sheltered hills protected from the fog of San Pablo Bay and most importantly, near the San Francisco grape market. Other natural factors which influence grapes and wines, namely, local wind currents, precipitation and its timing, and the general topography of Sonoma reminded him of the high quality vineyards in Hungary.

At first he bought a parcel of sixteen acres called "Vineyard Farm" which had been planted in 1834 by Salvadore Vallejo. The land was chosen by Vallejo because a creek was nearby. Mission grapes had almost always been planted on the banks of streams so that the roots would have constant moisture. It was believed that this was essential for productive yields. Haraszthy's past experience had taught him the fallacy of this practice. The superior grapes of his homeland were often planted on soil of near desert dryness. Scorning water and derisive comments by local growers, he planted his vines on the sloping hillside above Sonoma Valley where only occasional rains would reach them and the roots would not rot. He was the first in California to demonstrate in a practical way how to produce quality wine from non-irrigated grapes. The effect of his demonstration has been likened by oenologists to that of the cotton gin in the South.

Haraszthy's son Attila who had been in charge of the vineyard at Crystal Springs, was now assigned the task of transporting cuttings to Sonoma. Among the first vines transplanted was the Zinfandel which found its new home more than congenial and became Haraszthy's particular favorite.

Land was cheap and Haraszthy extended his holdings until, a few years later, he owned more than 6,000 acres. His vineyards alone were to cover over 400 acres. They soon ran up the foothills and sides of the Mayacamas Mountains to the ridge that separates Sonoma from Napa County. The soil was reddish ochre and highly mineralized. Numerous yellow and white sulphur springs of about eightly degrees in temperature, known to have salubrious effects, dotted the area.

Haraszthy named his new domain Buena Vista (Széptáj or Beautiful View again) and on an elevation within the sight of the Mayacamas and the waves of San Pablo Bay he built one of the finest houses in the Bay area. It was a white, Pompeian-style mansion with exquisite formal gardens in the front, all enclosed by an ornamental fence. A finely graveled concourse led up to it. In the following years it was the scene of many brilliant balls and social gatherings.

In the development of Buena Vista one could see Haraszthy at his enthusiastic best. He not only planted vines and more vines, but he also induced his friends to settle around him and follow his example. By the end of 1857 he had more than tripled the total grape acreage of Sonoma Valley. In that single year he had planted 80,000 vines on about 118 acres. Of these more than two-thirds were planted for his friends—among whom were Charles Krug, Emile Dreser, Jacob Grundlach and others who under his tutelage all became skilled growers and outstanding wine producers. Krug later crossed the mountains into Napa County to found a famous winery of his own. Dresel and Grundlach encouraged by Haraszthy experimented with German imports and methods.

Haraszthy built his first winery building of native stones in the summer of 1857 and not long after he followed it with a larger one. These two buildings are still in use today. Behind the buildings he cut a 100 foot tunnel, for a storage cellar, deep into the limestone hillside. This kept an ideal, cool, year around, constant temperature which helped the wine to mature with less danger of spoilage. The original tunnel was greatly expanded at the end of 1858 to store the increased production. Construction and cultivation were cheap, for Haraszthy's favorite laborers were Chinese who were paid $8.00 per month in cash wages and board. Haraszthy vigorously championed the cause of the Chinese against bitter and vociferous opposition and he urged all his friends to employ them. White labor demanded a minimum of $30.00 and board, and Indian and Mexican workers were far less industrious and dependable than the Chinese. In spite of his advocacy of liberal and humanitarian principles, Haraszthy had no hesitation in using his labor force under if not slave-like, certainly serf-like conditions, benevolent as he may have seemed.

One of Haraszthy's important innovations was his adoption of redwood for storage casks. The shortage of oak lumber and the high cost of imported oak made him experiment. Redwood proved to be a more than adequate replacement for the traditional oak, and its use for barrels quickly spread.

Activity at Buena Vista was intense. By the end of 1858 Haraszthy had more than a hundred imported grape varieties under cultivation. He was making progress toward the realization of his grand design. He envisioned Buena Vista as the great laboratory in which he would experiment with vines and soil, perfecting practical techniques. His indirect influence had become widespread. He sent cuttings of his vines all over the state and he offered thousands of rooted vines for sale. The inquiries and orders swamped his staff. Curious and interested visitors from all over came to the valley to watch his Chinese workers plow the soil, prune the vines, and excavate more tunnels, often working in moonlight if the heat of the day was too oppressive. Many newspaper reports and magazine articles were written on the miracle performed at Buena Vista: the production of sweeter fruit with finer flavor than any produced by irrigation. The little town of Sonoma became not only the central distributing point of European vines but also the fount of knowledge in viticultural matters.

In the annual State Fair in 1858 Haraszthy entered competition for the first time and won first prize. In 1859 he again took the top prize. General Vallejo who until then had had the field more or less to himself had to be satisfied with second prize. The friendly rivalry between the two neighbors grew with the years and culminated in a happy event. In 1863 Sonoma was the scene of the social highlight of the year when the Haraszthys and Vallejos joined in a double wedding. Attila and Árpád Haraszthy married the beautiful twin daughters of General Vallejo, Natalie and Jovita.

The years 1858-1861 further established Haraszthy's preeminence as a leading vintner. He organized and was chairman of the California Viticultural Society and, responding to an urgent demand for a competent guide, the State Agricultural Society asked him to prepare a paper on the history of wine in California and on preferred techniques. Haraszthy's monograph *Report on Grapes and Wines in California* became, and for many years remained, the best guide to practical viticulture in print. But his crowning achievement was still ahead of him.

The rapid but uncoordinated development in viticulture created chaotic conditions. Haraszthy suggested to the legislature that the State appoint a commission to study the methods used elsewhere and to collect choice varieties of vines and fruit trees. Agricultural interests and the press heartily endorsed the idea and the receptive assembly and senate quickly concurred and authorized Governor John G. Downey to appoint three commissioners, among them Haraszthy. He convinced the Governor that collecting the choicest vines and cuttings of Europe would be most profitable for California. The ink was hardly dry on the Governor's signature when on June 11, 1861, he sailed from San Francisco. His mission had the blessing of the legislature but he paid his own bills trusting to be reimbursed on his return. In New York he arranged with Harper & Brothers to publish a diary of his travels including a detailed account of the methods used in the best vineyards and wineries of Europe.

Árpád, who had been studying in Paris and latterly in the champagne district learning the manufacture of champagne, joined him. Haraszthy and Árpád spent over five months in Europe visiting nearly every important wine producing region. Curiously they did not include Hungary on their itinerary. Haraszthy gave no explanation, not even an inkling. Wherever they went they consulted the best authorities and took copious notes. He placed orders at Heidelberg, Genoa, Bordeaux, Malaga, and he authorized American consuls to send him additional shipments from Portugal, Greece, and Egypt. Upon his return to Buena Vista in December 1861 he immediately drafted his report and recommendations to the legislature. It included the amazing statement: "...I have purchased in different parts of Europe 100,000 vines, embracing about 1,400 varieties and small lots of choice almonds, olives, figs, pomegranates, Italian chestnuts, oranges, and lemons—enough to propagate by grafts."[7]

Here, in one massive importation were the products accumulated from a thousand years of wine culture in Central, Western, and Mediterranean Europe. It was an unparalleled feat.

Haraszthy concluded his report suggesting a method for the distribution of vines and trees to vintners and horticulturists and requesting reimbursement for the cost of the collection and shipping. "...I ask no remuneration for my personal services as Commissioner; on the contrary I feel proud of the honor and I will be richly remunerated if I have done any service to my adopted country."[8]

While the legislature debated his proposals and the appropriation for reimbursement, which took several months, Haraszthy completed the manuscript of his book *Grape Culture, Wines and*

Wine Making, with Notes upon Agriculture and Horticulture. It was published by Harper & Brothers in New York in 1862.

The book was eagerly received and widely read. It received rave notices. The reviewer for *Harper's New Monthly Magazine* wrote: "Few more readable books of travel have been produced than that portion of the work which describes his personal experiences and observations." A quote from a contemporary literary review: "It deserves to be ranked among the minor, accidental masterpieces of our national literature; in pace and gusto it recalls as much as anything, the lesser novels of Jules Verne." For a long time it was considered by many viticulturists the most authoritative book of its kind.

In the spring of 1862 the Civil War was raging, and the atmosphere in Sacramento was anything but favorable to Haraszthy. Partisan feelings ran high. The legislature was controlled by Republicans and Union Democrats, and Haraszthy was suspected of being a "copperhead" because of his affiliation with the so-called Peace Democrats. His opponents bluntly charged that he had devised the whole project as an expensive personal junket. The same treatment was accorded his six point program aimed at improving grape culture in California. On April 2, 1862, the senate shelved the bill for the appropriation as well as for the distribution of his collection. The failure of the state to preserve and propagate the vines resulted in a tremendous loss, for while Haraszthy made a valiant effort by traveling all over the state demonstrating, the primitive method of distribution resulted in general confusion. The valuable vines were scattered. Many were lost, others abandoned after growers tired of experimenting with them.

The action of the legislature was roundly denounced by many. Governor Downey protested that it was ". . .the vilest outrage ever perpetrated." It was also a serious blow to Haraszthy's vision, not to mention his finances. He had spent well over $10,000 on this venture. But he did not brood over the setback. His Buena Vista ranch was the leading vine center of the state, each year expanding its acreage and production, and in the fall of 1862 the activity was particularly feverish. Árpád, back from France, was put in charge of the wine production. Also, the first two casks of Zinfandel wine were tasted. Haraszthy was overjoyed. It had been eleven years since the first cuttings were received from General Mészáros. Additional storage cellars were dug to accommodate the growing production and the most modern equipment was installed for the manufacture of wine and brandy. The growth potential of Buena Vista seemed unlimited.

All this did not escape the watchful eyes of the banking interests in San Francisco which were always on the alert for promising investments. It was William C. Ralston, the founder and head of the Bank of California, who made the overture to Haraszthy. Billy Ralston and Haraszthy had been cronies during the panic of 1855. Ralston's spectacular career in many respects paralleled Haraszthy's own. Within two decades they had both attained the pinnacle of accomplishment, followed by a dramatic fall. (Later they even perished in the same manner—drowning under mysterious circumstances.) The verdict of history on Ralston is double-edged. On the one hand he is viewed as an unscrupulous, predatory, economic exploiter who looted the Bank of California to the tune of ten million dollars, an enormous sum in 1875. He ruthlessly eliminated competition in the Comstock Lode and his manipulations corrupted state and municipal governments. On the other hand his contribution to California's growth and prosperity was extraordinary. He put together railroads, steamship and telegraph companies, woolen mills, sugar refineries, cigar and furniture factories. He erected the finest theater on the West Coast and he was among the first regents of the University of California. But Ralston was Haraszthy's nemesis.

The development of Buena Vista was a costly operation. The investment in the expanding acreage, the new equipment, the costly venture to Europe, and the slow return from the sale of the large collection of vines and trees severely drained his liquid resources. The vineyards were heavily mortgaged and the interest rates were high. Additional capital to carry out further plans was difficult to raise.

When Ralston approached Haraszthy he proposed to relieve him of the mortgages, incorporate Buena Vista, infuse fresh capital, put the whole operation on a sound financial basis, and make it the major wine producer of the entire country. Pressed as he was and attractive as Ralston's proposal sounded, Haraszthy did not assent. He was still considering a plan he had conceived as early as 1860: to subdivide his lands into ten, twenty, and thirty acre plots, set out with choice vines. He intended to care for them for three years and then sell the tracts for about $200 an acre to the workers on his estate, to friends, and to other interested parties. When he ultimately agreed to Ralston's offer he still visualized a cooperative organization. The original concept was soon abandoned. Instead of small independent vineyards, a corporation, hiring Chinese and other day laborers to work the vineyards, was created. The Buena Vista Vinicultural Society was from the start a corporation with all its characteristics. Its capitalization was $600,000 divided into 6,000 shares. Haraszthy transferred Buena Vista to the corporation. He was paid 2,600 shares and his mortgages were taken over by the Society. He was also appointed superintendent and paid a salary to direct the operation.

The new enterprise got off to an auspicious start. Under Haraszthy's expert guidance both production and sales increased rapidly. New facilities were built particularly for the production of champagne. Interest in BVVS was intense. Fabulous accounts of it with detailed descriptions of Haraszthy's elegant Pompeian residence and its formal gardens appeared in several journals.

The first problem to cast its shadow on the future was the first batch of champagne from Buena Vista. After lengthy experiments Árpád succeeded in producing about 100 bottles which were highly satisfactory. The second trial run was equally good and the samples won an honorary diploma at the State Fair. It was an encouraging start and Árpád was ordered to proceed on a large scale. Ten thousand bottles were produced and they proved to be dismal. The wine had lost all its good qualities. Árpád attributed the fiasco to the absence of proper temperature control; the fires had not been correctly maintained. To remedy this he took his blankets and slept in the fermenting room for three months, keeping the fires going during the nights. In 1864 when Árpád Haraszthy analyzed the causes and believed he had found a solution to the problem, he was unable to convince the trustees to let him carry on. Árpád's failure created friction and pressure. Ralston, with the financier's drive for quick profits, had no patience for the deliberate, painstaking approach of Árpád. Ralston demanded action and results. Árpád, as quietly resolute as his father was impulsively brilliant, would not stand for the pressure Ralston applied. He resigned and continued his experiments on his own and he ultimately became famous as a premier champagne maker.

Haraszthy somehow felt himself responsible for the champagne fiasco, and annoyed by Ralston's behavior, undertook to foot the bills himself. They were substantial. Ralston, incensed by Árpád's independence, nursed his grudge against Haraszthy and in the end succeeded in forcing him out of the Society.

There were several factors which slowed down the projected growth of the Society: lagging demand, increasing costs, and an excise tax on wine and brandy imposed by Congress in 1865. Because of a shortage of liquid capital the directors were forced to suspend the payment of dividends. Haraszthy found himself in a desperate struggle to steer the Society through its financial crisis. Ralson, using the leverage of the Bank of California, was determined to force him out. He dismissed the long term potential of Haraszthy's projects as overly risky and he instigated news articles and rumors charging Haraszthy with extravagantly visionary experimentation. The attacks became so frequent and malicious that the directors issued a statement defending Haraszthy's management and challenging anyone to prove the charges. Although he was vindicated Haraszthy felt his usefulness at Buena Vista was at an end. He had no stomach for a power struggle with Ralston. In total frustration he resigned his position and left the Society in 1866.

Not unduly dismayed by the setback Haraszthy threw himself into a whirlwind campaign of organizing the winemakers into a tightly knit group. He also engaged in serious social planning. In a perceptive analysis which he published in the *Alta California* he advocated an elaborate plan to attract European immigration to California which he considered essential for the state's expanding economy. All the while he did not neglect his beloved grapes. He took over the management of a small vineyard nearby which his son Attila had bought for his mother. But here too he suffered a serious blow. A boiler exploded in his distillery and to escape the scalding steam, he jumped from a second story window, badly twisting his ankle. For many weeks he got around on crutches. This mishap was just a forerunner of other disastrous turns. His investments on the San Francisco stockmarket declined. His notes were called and his bankers were not too accommodating. Soon after, one of his wine cellars containing vintages of two years as well as his cooperage were destroyed by fire. This last loss alone was overwhelming. Misfortune seemed to dog him.

It did not take long for Haraszthy to recover his resiliency, but he appeared to have grown weary of the California scene after the series of lost battles. He was fifty-six years old but with the restless energy of his youthful days he once again dared to break new ground.

For many years he had followed with fascination the filibustering expeditions of William Walker and his reign as president of Nicaragua. He had also been intrigued by the reports of Count Wass, his ex-partner in the Eureka Refinery, about the vast natural resources of Central America. After making preliminary inquiries and negotiating for trading rights with the government, he sailed for Nicaragua. His wife and his son Géza accompanied him. Upon surveying the land, his natural talent for promoting the unexploited potential triggered his usual quota of grandiose plans for the future.

First he bought a sugar plantation at Corinto in partnership with others and soon gained a concession from the government to develop an additional 100,000 acres of choice land around it. By clearing the new land and planting new canes he made it the largest plantation in the country. His next move was the construction of a rum distillery and he was granted an export monopoly by the grateful government. He also designed and built a sawmill to cut and dress mahogany and other valuable hardwoods found in the vast forests of his new "domain" which he named Hacienda San Antonio. Another of his projects was the utilization of native textile fibres. He designed improved machinery for their cleansing and treatment and projected a flourishing export trade. He lived now in the baronial style of a great plantation owner.

In July 1868 an unexpected calamity occurred. His wife, Eleonora, came down with yellow fever and died. To overcome his grief he buried himself in work. In December 1868 he returned to San Francisco to purchase machinery and other equipment and also to charter a ship with which he was going to inaugurate general trade between San Francisco and the ports of Central America. On January 22, 1869, he sailed from San Francisco for the last time. His father, the old General, although seventy-nine by then, insisted on going along. The General's wife and Haraszthy's daughter Ottilia also went with them. The humid, tropical climate however did not agree with the General and he left the plantation early in May to return to California. However, he never reached San Francisco, for he died on board ship. And his son died in the same year.

A long and laudatory obituary appeared in the *Alta California:*

Colonel Agoston Haraszthy

As one of the pioneers of California, the important services rendered to the State by Colonel Haraszthy demand more than a passing notice. All doubt as to his death is now removed by a letter from a member of his family, dated San Antonio, Nicaragua, July 22. The writer says: "Father on the 6th of July, left the house to go to a new landing (where they were putting up a sawmill) to meet a Mr. Lewis. But not finding him, he spoke to the workmen, saying the mill was too far from the river, and would have been better on the other side. He then rode to the river, tied his mule, spread his oilcloth coat on the ground, rolled up his other coat and must have laid down on it for a time. From thence his footsteps were traced to a large tree, the limbs of which reach to the other side of the river. About the middle of the stream a large limb was found to be broken, and at the same place, a few days before, an alligator dragged a cow into the stream from the bank. We must conclude that father tried to cross the river by the tree, and that losing his balance he fell, grasping the broken limb. and then the alligator must have drawn him down forever.

The obituary then continued, reciting in great detail Haraszthy's deeds.[9]

Haraszthy's body was never found. The conjecture of how he met his death is the only clue to the mystery of his disappearance. His death like his life and extraordinary career was as dramatic as his flamboyant imagination could have presaged.

The following excerpt is from the Congressional Record of the first session of the 91st Congress (1969) on the occasion of the 100th anniversary of his death:

"...Too often we overlook those true men of vision whose foresight has so profoundly influenced our lives...California has put Count Haraszthy on its cultural maps and there is no doubt he belongs there. In a very significant way he put California on the nation's economic and gourmet maps. . . ."

Born aristocrat, yet frontiersman at heart, he was equally at home in the elegant ducal salons of Europe or the gaudy

nouveaux riches of San Francisco and the savage wilderness of the West. Playing Bach and Beethoven while enforcing the law of the frontier, he was a soldier, law student, author, legislator, town builder, sheriff, metallurgist, land promoter, steamboater, saw- mill operator, wagon train master, politician, lobbyist, humanist, visionary, but most important of all he was the "Father of Califor- nia's Viticulture."

Perhaps the most ingenuous tribute paid him is the dedication in an old book on vine culture in California:

"This book is dedicated to the pioneer vine growers of Califor- nia, the most colorful of whom was Count Agoston Haraszthy, born in Hungary in 1812, whence he fled politics to become a resident of California from 1849 to 1868.

"He died in Nicaragua in 1869, supposedly eaten by crocodiles.[10]

"He was always a gentleman, as far as is known. He is now referred to as the father of modern wine growing in the Western world."

NOTES

1. Agoston Haraszthy, *Utazas Éjszakamerikaban* [Travels in North America] 2 vols., (Pest: Gustav Heckenast, 1844), 2:14-15.
2. Ibid., 1:121.
3. Ibid., 2:281-282.
4. Verne S. Pease, "Agoston Haraszthy," *Proceedings of the Wisconsin Historical Society* (1906):240-241.
5. The Derleth novel is the third in his series of the Sac Prairie Saga. It is an epic tale of the flight of Count Augustin Brogmar, an intrepid adventurer, from his ancestral estate in Hungary to the wilderness of Wisconsin. In this story of the frontier days, Haraszthy receives a fresh lease on life in the character of Count Brogmar. Mark Schorer's hero, Count Karanszcy, and his pioneering deeds is a thinly disguised take-off on Haraszthy.
6. *U.S. Circuit Court Record,* Sept. 19, 1857 to April 24, 1861; *San Francisco Evening Bulletin, Daily Alta California, San Francisco Herald,* June 1, 1857 to July 1861; Janos Xantus, *Levelei Ejszakamerikabol* [Letters from North America] (Pest, 1857), 170-175; R.H. Dillon, *J. Ross Browne: Confidential Agent in Old California* (Norman, Oklahoma: University of Oklahoma Press, 1965), pp. 140-143; Thomas H. Pauly, "J. Ross Browne," *California Historical Society Quarterly,* Summer 1972; D. M. Goodman, *A Western Panorama, 1875: the travels, writings and influence of J. Ross Browne* (Glendale, Calif., 1966), pp. 95-117; Brian McGinty, *Haraszthy at the Mint* (Los Angeles: Dawson, 1975). This last reference is a painstaking research by a descendant of Haraszthy refuting the Bancroft version of the case.
7. Agoston Haraszthy, *Grape Culture, Wines and Wine Making* (New York: Harper & Brothers, 1862), pp. xv-xxii.
8. *Appendices to the Journals of the California Legislature,* Session 13, 1862: p. 29.
9. *Alta California,* Aug. 27, 1869.
10. There are no crocodiles in Central America. Probably caymans (alligators) was meant.

BIBLIOGRAPHY

HARASZTHY IN HUNGARY

Barany, George. *Stephen Széchenyi and the Awakening of Hungarian Nationalism, 1791-1842.* Princeton: Princeton University Press, 1960.

Eckhart, Ferenc. *Magyarország története* (History of Hungary). Budapest: Kaldor Book Publishers, 1933.

Fenyö, Istvan. *Két évtized* (Two Decades). Budapest: Magvetö, 1968.

Haraszthy, Árpád. *The Haraszthy Family.* Manuscript, 1886. Bancroft Library, University of California, Berkeley, Calif.

Kosáry, Dominic G. *A History of Hungary.* Cleveland-New York: The Benjamin Franklin Bibliophile Society, 1941.

Macartney, C.A. *The Habsburg Empire, 1790-1918.* London: Weidenfeld and Nicolson, 1968.

——————*Hungary, a Short History.* Chicago: Aldine Publishing, 1962.

Molnár, Erik, ed. *Magyarország története* (History of Hungary). 2 vols. Budapest: Gondolat Könyvkiadó, 1964.

Nagy, Iván, *Magyarország családai* (Families of Hungary), 5 vols. Pest: 1859.

Paget, John. *Hungary and Transylvania.* 2 vols. Philadelphia: Lea and Blanchard, 1850.

Pivany, Eugene. *Magyarok és Északamerika.* (Hungarians and North America). Budapest: Officina, 1944.

Trócsányi, Zsolt, *Wesselényi Miklós.* Budapest: Akadémiai Kiadó, 1965.

Mályusz, Elemér. "A reformkor nemzedéke" (The Generation of the Age of Reform) *Századok* (Centuries) LVII-LVIII.

Sztáray, Zoltán. "Haraszty Ágoston" *Uj Látohatár* (New Perspective). VII. Budapest, 1964.

HARASZTHY IN WISCONSIN

Cole, H. E. *Standard History of Sauk County.* Chicago: Western Historical Society, 1880.

Canfield, W. H. *Outline Sketches of Sauk County,* Baraboo, 1861.

Gregory, J. G. *Southwestern Wisconsin.* 2 vols. Chicago: S. J. Clarke Publishing Co., 1922.

Derleth, August. *Restless is the River.* New York: Scribner's Sons, 1934.

Kellogg, L. P. *The Story of Wisconsin.* New York: Barnes & Noble, 1945.

Pease, Verne S. "Agoston Haraszthy" in *Proceedings of the Wisconsin State Historical Society,* 1906.

Wisconsin, A Guide to the Badger State. New York: Duell, Sloan & Pierce, 1941.

Dictionary of Wisconsin biography. Madison: Wisconsin State Historical Society, 1960.

Schorer, Mark. *A House Too Old.* New York: Reynal and Hitchcock, 1935.
Collections of the Wisconsin State Historical Society, Vols. 2, 8, 12, 14.
Madison, Wisconsin.
Wisconsin Magazine of History. Madison: Wisconsin State Historical
Society. Vols. 2, 3, 6, 9, 10, 11, 12, 23.

HARASZTHY IN CALIFORNIA

Bancroft, Hubert H. *History of California.* Vol. VII. San Francisco: A.L.
Bancroft & Co.
_____ *California Inter Pocula.* San Francisco: A. L. Bancroft & Co.
Bean, Walton E. *California, An interpretive history.* New York: McGraw Hill
Co., 1968.
Bieber, R. P. ed. *Southern Trails to California.* Glendale, Calif.: Arthur H.
Clark Co., 1937.
Caughey, John W. *California.* New York: Prentice-Hall, 1940.
Clover, Sam T. *A Pioneer Heritage.* Los Angeles, Calif.: Saturday Night
Publishing Co., 1932.
Dillon, Richard H. *J. Ross Browne: Confidential Agent in Old California,*
Norman, Okla.: University of Oklahoma Press, 1965.
Goodman, David M. *A Western Panorama, 1849-1875: the travels, writings
and influence of J. Ross Browne.* Glendale, Calif.: Arthur H. Clark Co.,
1966.
Gregory, Tom. *History of Sonoma County.* Los Angeles: Historic Record
Co., 1911.
Guinn, J. M. *History of the State of California and Biographical Record of
Sacramento Valley.* Chicago: Historic Record Co., 1906.
Fredericksen, Paul. *The Authentic Haraszthy Story* (Reprinted from *Wines
and Vines*). San Francisco: Wine Advisory Board, 1947.
Jones, Idwal. *Vines in the Sun: A Journey through the California Vineyards.*
New York: Morrow, 1949.
Hayes, Benjamin. *Scrapbooks. Notes on California Affairs.* Bancroft Library,
Berkeley, Calif.
McGrew, C. A. *City of San Diego and San Diego County.* Chicago: The
American Historical Society, 1922.
McKittrick, M. M. *Vallejo, Son of California.* Portland, Ore.: Binford and
Mort, 1924.
Menefee, C. A. *Historical and Descriptive Sketchbook of Napa, Sonoma, Lake,
and Mendocino.* Napa: Reporter Publishing House, 1873.
Newmark, Harris. *Sixty Years in Southern California, 1853-1913.* 2d. rev. ed.
New York: Houghton Mifflin Co., 1930.
Murray, W. H. *The Builders of a Great City: San Francisco's Representative
Men.* 2 vols. San Francisco: San Francisco Journal, 1891.
Powell, H. M. T. *The Santa Fe Trail to California.* Los Angeles: Grabhorn
Press, 1931.

Roske, Ralph J. *Everyman's Eden, A History of California*. New York: Mac-Millan, 1968.

San Francisco Almanac for 1859. San Francisco: Daily Alta California, 1859.

Smythe, William E. *History of San Diego*. San Diego: The History Company, 1908.

HARASZTHY IN VITICULTURE

Adams, Leon D. *The Wines of America*. Boston: Houghton-Mifflin Co., 1973.

Amerine, Maynard A. *Wine, an introduction for Americans*. Berkeley: University of California Press, 1977.

Atherton, Gertrude. *Golden Gate County*. New York: Duell, Sloan and Pierce, 1945. XI (American Folkways, ed. by Erskine Caldwell).

Balzer, Robert L. *California's Best Wines*. Los Angeles: The Ward Ritchie Press, 1948.

Blumberg, Robert S. and Hannum, Hurst. *The Fine Wines of California*. New York: Doubleday, 1971.

Bynum, Lindley. *California Wines. How to Enjoy Them*. Los Angeles: Homer H. Boelter Lith., 1955.

California Wine Country. Menlo Park: Lane Books, 1968.

"California as a Vineland" *Atlantic Monthly*. XIII. May 1864.

Carosso, Vincent P. *The California Wine Industry, 1830-1895*. Berkeley: University of California Press, 1951.

Donohue, Joan M. "Agostin Haraszthy: A Study in Creativity" in *California Historical Society Quarterly*. XLVIII. No. 2. June 1969.

Fisher, M.F. *The Story of Wine in California*. Berkeley: University of California Press, 1962.

Grossman, Harold J. *Grossman's Guide to Wines, Spirits and Beers*. New York: Scribner's, 1964.

Hyatt, Hart T. *Hyatt's Handbook of Grape Culture*. San Francisco: H.H. Bancroft and Co., 1867.

Haraszthy, Agoston. "Report on grapes and wine of California by Col. A. Haraszthy of Buena Vista, Sonoma County, Calif." *Transactions of the California State Agricultural Society during the year 1858*.

_____ *Grape Culture, Wines and Wine-making. With notes upon Agriculture and Horticulture*. New York: Harper & Bros, 1862.

Haraszthy, Árpád. *California Grapes and Wines*. San Francisco: Pub. 1888.

_____ "Early Viticulture in Sonoma" in *Sonoma County and Russian River Valley*. San Francisco, 1888.

_____ "Wine Making in California" *Overland Monthly*. San Francisco. December 1871.

Jones, Idwal. "Among the vintners" *Westways*. Vol. 27, no. 9. Beverly Hills, Calif. September 1935.

_____ "He planted the Zinfandel" *Westways*. Vol. 34, no. 9. Beverly Hills, Calif. September 1942.

Lichine, Alexis. *Encyclopedia of Wines and Spirits*. New York: Knopf, 1967.

Nesfield, David C. *The Vineland of the West*. San Francisco: 1883.

Silver, J. S. "The Vineyards of California" *Overland Monthly*. October 1868.

Simon, Andre C. *Wines of the World*. New York: McGraw Hill, 1967.

Schoonmaker, Frank. *Encyclopedia of Wines*. New York: Hastings House, 1970.

Stevenson, Robert L. *Silverado Squatters*. London: Chatto and Windus, 1883.

Stoll, Horatio F. "Agoston Haraszthy's Eventful Career" *Wines and Vines*. XVIII. January 1937.

_____ "The Development of the California Wine Industry" *Argonaut*, CXII, March 16, 1934.

_____ "Pioneer Winemakers of the Historic Sonoma District" *Wines and Vines*, XVIII, May 1937.

Sullivan, Charles L. "A Viticultural Mystery Solved: The Historical Origins of Zinfandel in California." *California History*. Summer 1978.

Sztáray, Zoltán. *Haraszthy Agoston, a kaliforniai szölökulture atyja* [A. H. Father of the California viticulture]. San Bernardino, Calif.: The Kossuth Foundation, 1964.

Wagner, P. M. *Wine Growers Guide*. New York: Knopf, 1965.

Waite, F.E. *Wines and Vines of California*. San Francisco: A. L. Bancroft & Co., 1889.

_____ "Wine-Making in California." *Harper's Magazine*. XXIX. June, 1864.

Xantus, János. *Levelek Ejszakamerikából* [Letters from North America]. Pest, 1858.

MISCELLANEOUS

Dictionary of American Biography. New York: Scribner's, 1932.

Challacombe, J. R. "Vintage California." *Westways*. Vol. 57, no. 11, Beverly Hills, Cal. November 1965.

Churchman, Evelyn. "Raisins of the sun." *California History Nugget*. Vol. 7, no. 2. Calif. State Dept. of Educ. Sacramento, Calif: Nov. 1939.

Eisen, Gustav. *The Raisin Industry*. San Francisco: H.S. Crocker & Co., 1890.

Evans, William E. "The Garra uprising: conflict between San Diego Indians and settlers in 1851." *California Historical Society Quarterly*. Vol. 45, no. 4, San Francisco, Dec. 1966.

Hart, James D. *A Companion to California*. New York: Oxford University Press, 1978.

U.S. Department of Agriculture Reports. 1871, 1872, 1873. California Department of Parks and Recreation. California Historical Landmarks. Sacramento, 1960.

Kende, Géza. *Magyarok Amerikában. Az amerikai magyarság története* [Hungarians in America. The History of American Hungarians, 1583-1926]. 2 vols. Cleveland, Ohio: Szabadság (Liberty), 1927.

Szinnyei, J. *Magyar irók élete éésmunkái* [Life and works of Hungarian writers]. Budapest, 1896.

Vasváry, E. *Lincoln's Hungarian Heroes. The Participation of Hungarians in the Civil War. 1861-65.* Washington, 1939.

Mészáros, Lazar. *Külfoldi levelezści* [Foreign correspondence]. Pest, 1866. 1866.

Cochran, Thomas C. and Miller, William. *The Age of Enterprise: A Social History of Industrial America.* New York: Harper & Row, 1961.

North, Douglass C. *The Economic Growth of the United States, 1790-1860.* Englewood Cliffs, N.J.: Prentice-Hall, 1961.

Schlesinger, Arthur M., Jr. *The Age of Jackson.* Boston: Little Brown & Co., 1945.

Turner, Frederick J. *The United States 1830-1850. The Nation and Its Sections.* New York: Henry Holt & Co., 1935.

Van Deusen, Glyndon G. *The Jacksonian Era, 1828-1848.* New York: Harper & Brothers, 1959.

White, Leonard D. *The Jacksonians: a Study in Administrative History, 1829-1861.* New York: MacMillan, 1954.

View of the ranch house and buildings of the Buena Vista Vinicultural Society at Sonoma, taken
by Muybridge in the 1870s.

General Charles Haraszthy, father of Agoston Haraszthy.

Arpad Haraszthy, third son of Agoston Haraszthy. Arpad was born at Futak, Hungary, in 1840 and died in San Francisco in 1900, full of honors as a viticulturist and as an early producer of California champagnes.

Eleanora, wife of Agoston Haraszthy.

Ho Po, a San Francisco labor contractor who furnished
Chinese workmen to the Buena Vista Winery.

Buena Vista Vineyard, 1865.

Buena Vista Vineyards; Plowing.

This picture, taken by Muybridge in the 1870s was captioned:
"Loading grapes, Buena Vista Vineyard."

Winery building at Buena Vista ranch, built in 1864 by Haraszthy. Here some of the vintages of the Buena Vista Vinicultural Society were pressed and aged; wine-storage tunnels led from its rear wall into the solid rock of a hillside. (Photo by S G. Morley, Berkeley, 1947)

One of six wine storage tunnels excavated by Chinese laborers under the direction of Colonel Agoston Haraszthy. The tunnels pierced the rock of a hillside at Buena Vista; and in front of each group of three, Haraszthy built a large stone winery. This view is from the interior of the first of the two stone wineries. The tunnel shown may have been dug as early as 1857, and certainly was in existence by 1862. In its days of greatest usefulness it probably held champagne. A cave-in has let daylight into the tunnel. (Photo by S. G. Morley, Berkeley, 1947.)

Labels of the Buena Vista Vinicultural Society, founded in 1863. The Sweet Muscatel and Vin de la Montagne labels were printed black on white paper. The El Dorado Claret label had a gold design and black printing on white paper.

GRAPE CULTURE,

WINES, AND WINE-MAKING.

WITH NOTES UPON

AGRICULTURE AND HORTICULTURE.

BY

A. HARASZTHY,

COMMISSIONER TO REPORT ON THE IMPROVEMENT AND CULTURE OF THE VINE IN
CALIFORNIA.

With Numerous Illustrations.

NEW YORK:

1862.

PREFACE.

I SUBMIT this work to the kind indulgence of the people of California.

The short time allowed me to complete a work of such magnitude and importance will, I hope, serve as a partial excuse for its defects.

To make a tour through a large portion of Europe—examine and collect information—select vines and trees—write the following work, with many of the extracts translated from eminent foreign authors and reports of scientific committees, I was allowed, including my journey to Europe and my return, but seven months and twenty-five days.

The task was augmented by extensive and necessary correspondence with government officials, scientific societies, and eminent writers.

During this time I have allowed myself little time for rest or recreation; and if I have succeeded in fulfilling my duty to my State and to her people, I shall feel myself amply rewarded.

I plead for a lenient judgment on the work on account of my defective English, being a native of Hungary, although a naturalized American citizen, which will, I hope, fully explain this unavoidable defect. That my readers will understand my meaning without difficulty is all that I dare hope.

The translations contained in the work were, in most cases, necessarily literal, and therefore presented difficulties not easily overcome.

With these explanations, the author presents his work to the agricultural public, sincerely hoping that future experience may not belie present promises, but that the matter upon which it treats may prove a valuable and an enduring source of wealth to the American horticulturist and farmer.   A. H.

BUENA VISTA, *Sonoma County, California.*

REPORT.

To the Honorable the Senate and Assembly of the State of California:

IN accordance with a joint resolution of the Assembly, adopted March 2d, 1861, and concurred in by the Senate, April 1st, 1861, authorizing and requesting his Excellency the Governor to appoint a commission to report to the next Legislature upon the ways and means best adapted to promote the improvement and culture of the grape-vine in California, I have the honor respectfully to report as follows:

Having been appointed by his Excellency the Governor, J. G. Downey, upon said commission, I first considered the best mode of fulfilling the duties imposed by the above resolution.

It became evident to me that the objects of the Legislature would be best secured by an examination of the different varieties of grapes, and the various modes of making wine, in the wine-growing countries of Europe, and I communicated this view to the Governor, and offered my services to proceed to Europe, if he should think it desirable. He approved my suggestion, and sanctioned the enterprise, and I at once proceeded on my journey. On my way I stopped at Washington, and was supplied by the Hon. W. H. Seward, Secretary of State for the United States, with a circular letter, directing the diplomatic agents of the United States in Europe to afford me such assistance as lay in their power in this important mission.

On my arrival in France, I opened a correspondence with the different imperial agricultural and horticultural societies, requesting them to furnish such information and letters of introduction as would facilitate my object. They responded with cheerfulness; and I was received with distinction, and afforded every opportunity for obtaining the information I required; in fact, I met with general courtesy wherever I went.

I visited various parts of France, the Netherlands, Holland, Rhenish Prussia, Bavaria, Nassau, Baden, Switzerland, Spain, Italy, and England. Various examinations confirmed my previous conviction that California is superior in all the conditions of soil, climate, and other natural advantages, to the most favored wine-producing districts of Europe, and that it actually has yielded considerably more per acre. All this State requires to produce a generous and noble wine is the varieties of grapes from which the most celebrated wines are made, and the same care and science in its manufacture. This conclusion is the result of a thorough investigation, and frequent consultations with many eminent men in Europe, who assured me that the quality of the grapes governs, in a great measure, the quality of the wine; a fact proved by many scientific experiments, showing that, even in the least favored localities, where common wines were ordinarily made, the finest and most costly wines had been produced by planting the best varieties of grape.

Having provided myself with analyses of the soil of California from various locations, it was not difficult to obtain a correct estimate of its average capacity as a wine-producing State. From all the information I have been able to get, our climate and soil are greatly in our favor.

In view of all these facts and the purpose of my mission, I determined to make arrangements to purchase a quantity of vines, and also to examine every celebrated wine-making establishment within the limits of my tour, so as to learn and describe the newest and best methods of making wine. I did not limit my observation and study to the manufactories alone, but procured the reports of scientific committees, appointed by different governments to investigate the subject by means of practical experiments, continued through a series of years. I also obtained the proceedings of the Congress assembled, by order of the government of France, for the purposes of comparison and consultation, and which was composed of the most scientific chemists and practical wine-makers. I availed myself of the reports of similar assemblies held annually in Germany, and of the newest and best works in various languages, written by able men, who had spent their lives in the business of vine culture and wine-making.

It is proper to remark here that I discovered that the countries through which I traveled possessed a lucrative trade by making raisins, drying figs and prunes, raising almonds, cultivating mulberry-trees for the sustenance of silk-worms, and, above all, producing sugar at enormous profits from the Sorgho, Imphee, and the sugar-beet; and I therefore thought it advisable to add to the more strict duties of my mission an investigation into these branches of industry, and to procure the best and newest works concerning them.

I was gratified to find that of all the countries through which I passed, not one possessed the same advantages that are to be found in California; and I am satisfied that even if the separate advantages of these countries could be combined in one, it would still be surpassed by this State when its now dormant resources shall be developed.

California can produce as noble and generous a wine as any in Europe; more in quantity to the acre, and without repeated failures through frosts, summer rains, hailstorms, or other causes.

The quantity of raisins, currants, figs, almonds, olives, and prunes which we could raise would surprise the most sanguine of our people. The mulberry and the silk-worm would occupy and give support to many industrious females, who have now no remunerative employment, in the rural districts; would aid the small farmer in his efforts to raise and educate a growing family, and would add largely to the wealth and revenue of the State.

In my opinion, no country can surpass this in raising the sugar-beet, Sorgho, and Imphee. There is no part of the world, except perhaps Africa, which can produce the same quantity of these commodities to the acre. The present mode of making sugar from these products is so simple that every farmer, at an expense of $30 for machinery, can manufacture enough for his own use, and have a considerable overplus each year for the market. The capitalist, too, may safely invest his money in this lucrative business, and enrich himself as well as the State.

The countries I visited in which these products were cultivated and manufactured derive from them a considerable revenue, as their statistics show; and there is no substantial obstacle to prevent the agriculturists of California from engaging in all the enterprises I have mentioned. The high price of labor here is more than counterbalanced by the greater value of land, and the enormous taxes on these productions in Europe. The development of these branches of industry would not only add to the wealth of the State, but it would also lead to a large immigration from Europe. Men conversant with these businesses have not hitherto migrated to California because they had no hope of suitable employment. Capitalists, ignorant of these resources of the State, have not considered the advantages they present for investment. Manufacturers who have grown wealthy in the older countries, having sons or junior partners, would gladly open branch-houses here as soon as it was known that they could purchase an ade-

B

quate supply of the raw material in this State. But it would be impossible to enumerate all the benefits which this State would derive from such an increased application of her agricultural capacity. Residents of California who have visited our plantations, vineyards, and farms, and who have attended our district and county fairs, may be able to appreciate these just anticipations.

European governments, well knowing the importance of agriculture and horticulture, appropriate large sums every year, in various ways, for the encouragement of these most important branches of their wealth. Agents are sent to all parts of the world to collect information, to report on new inventions and ameliorations, and to purchase new varieties of vines, trees, seeds, etc. Botanical or experimental gardens are kept, where the plants, vines, or fruit-trees are propagated, and then sold to the people for cost price, or given free of charge to each and every community, according to population, for distribution among its landholders. Scientific and practical men are employed at high salaries as officers of agriculture and horticulture, whose duty it is to make experiments in all their various branches. The magnificent agricultural and horticultural schools, with their experimental gardens, costs some States hundreds of thousands of dollars per annum, and their statesmen frankly admit that money could not be more profitably expended. It can also be shown by statistics that those States which have expended most money in the encouragement of these departments of industry are now the wealthiest and most powerful, and their people the least in want. I would respectfully recommend that a law be passed appropriating money for the purchase of land for a propagating and an experimental garden, and creating the office of director to supervise the garden; and also the appropriation of a sum to purchase, from year to year, seeds, vines, etc.; and for other necessary expenses in maintaining said garden. In this connection, I would respectfully draw your attention to the fact that, by late treaties with Japan and China, an opportunity is presented to us to penetrate into those countries, which have been secluded for centuries. It is well known that many fruits and plants are raised there which might be of great advantage if introduced into this State. A thorough examination of those countries would probably bring to light some products which have not been thought of here. To leave such inquiries to private enterprise would be a tardy mode of realizing the object. I doubt if half a century would accomplish, by private means, what might speedily be attained by official investigation. No private individual, however wealthy, would have the same facilities to investigate and procure seeds and plants as an agent authorized by his government. This is the case in civilized Europe. How much more necessary is such a prestige in semi-civilized countries? The passage of a law for the above purposes may be opposed on the ground that we have a national garden at Washington, but it is well known that the few shrubs and seeds we receive from thence are too often dry and useless.

California ought to propagate only such vines, fruits, seeds, etc., as are congenial to her soil and climate, and in large quantities, so that our citizens can be promptly supplied. The Patent Office represents too varied interests, climates, and soils, to do much good to us here. One might as well say that California needs no Governor, Legislature, or Judiciary, as that our public affairs might be administered from Washington; and, in fact, it would be easier to govern us from Washington, than for the Patent Office to supply what we want for the speedy development of our agricultural and horticultural resources.

In my travels I endeavored to induce capitalists to come among us and establish business places, to purchase the grapes from the small producers as in Europe, and to erect manufactories for making wine and extracting sugar from Sorgho, beet-root, and Imphee. I also urged the formation of a joint-stock company, with a capital of a million dollars, for the planting of vines, olives, almonds, mulberries, etc., in the southern part of the State. The prospect for the consummation of these enterprises is favorable, and especially if the apprehensions of a foreign war should subside.

Whenever there was an opportunity to get an article about California and its immense resources in an influential newspaper, I embraced it, and many government journals heralded our advantages by publishing the letters your commissioner had written to their officials. Permit me to say here that in no way can the object of rapidly populating our State be more effectually accomplished than by authorized agents traveling in Europe, not for the direct purpose of inducing emigration, but of noting the progress of agricultural and manufacturing pursuits. These agents would come in contact with all classes of persons; questions would be eagerly asked, and opportunities be thus afforded to publish the advantages California possesses. Coming from an official source, the information would be credited, newspapers would refer to it, and, with the aid of the reports of our "State Agricultural Society" (which I was fortunate enough to possess), these authorized statements would be authenticated by the enumerated premiums and descriptions from visiting committees. It excited surprise that a State so young and so isolated should have already such wealth of agriculture and horticulture as I proved; and this surprise among Europeans is not so wonderful, as California was there known principally for its gold. Even our Eastern brethren were astonished when I showed from our reports the extraordinary productiveness of our soil and the salubrity of our climate. The appropriations made by the Legislature for the printing of the proceedings of the "State Agricultural Society" have, and will continue to bring back many times their amount. It would be well to distribute these evidences of our resources in such a manner as would reach more directly the people in the East and in Europe. Books sent to other agricultural societies generally fail to reach the public, being mostly retained in their libraries; but if they were sent to the editors of prominent newspapers, they would receive a much wider circulation.

I have purchased in different parts of Europe 100,000 vines, embracing about 1400 varieties; small lots of choice almonds, olives, oranges, lemons, figs, pomegranates, and Italian chestnuts —enough to propagate from by grafts. The majority of the grape-vines I have engaged I have seen bearing. From those countries which I was unable to visit I ordered, through our consuls (to whom I remitted the necessary funds), such products as I thought necessary, and I have no doubt they will be forwarded in time to be dispatched from Havre with the others. My contracts were made, in all places, in presence of the United States consul, leaving the money with him to be paid when the vines, etc., were delivered, and instructing the consuls to send them, so as to arrive in Havre on or a few days before the 1st of December, 1861. A gardener whom I employed will attend to their proper shipment, take charge of them on the voyage, and repack them in New York, where arrangements have been made with Wells, Fargo, & Co., for their farther transportation to San Francisco, under the care and supervision of the gardener. All necessary precautions have been taken, and I am confident they will arrive in the very best order. They are expected to reach San Francisco by the steamer due on the 23d of January, 1862. As I do not know the exact freight and expenses, I am not able to state the amount of cost and charges to your honorable body, but will do so as soon as possible.

It may not be irrelevant here to mention the fact that in California, as well as in the Eastern States, the public mistrust the purity of California made wines in the hands of merchants. Whether merchants do or do not adulterate the wine, such doubts injure its character, and restrict its sale greatly. Therefore, to insure confidence, and prevent such adulterations, I would respectfully submit whether it might not be a wise policy to pass an act appointing a general agent for the State, who should reside in San Francisco, and to whom the wine-producers could send their wines to be sold; the agent to sell the wine at the prices fixed by the manufacturer, with the proprietor's label on the bottles, or, if in barrels, with his name attached thereto. This agent, so appointed, to receive from the owners of all wines or brandies sold a commission, to be fixed by law, and not to exceed the commissions usually received by merchants; the agent to defray the expense of office and cellar out of the commissions he may receive. The law creating said office might also impose heavy fines and confiscation of the liquor belonging to any individual who should send for sale adulterated articles. Such an office would be no burden to the State nor to the wine-growers, as it would be optional with them to send their wines to this officer or dispose of them in any other way. Every producer, however, would find it to his advantage to avail himself of this medium, as he would meet a ready sale, and pay no more than the usual commissions, while he would aid in preventing frauds, and thus create confidence in the genuineness of our wines. The agent would have to be strictly impartial. All the samples should be indifferently exposed and accessible to purchasers, who could select the wines best suited to their tastes. The agent should be required to give ample bonds for the faithful and impartial performance of his duty, and for the prompt payment of all receipts on account of sales.

This plan would, I believe, restore confidence, and be at least a check upon poisoning our people by our own productions.

His Excellency the Governor has directed me to propagate the vines expected to arrive here from Europe at Sonoma, and hold them and the increase subject to the future disposition of the Legislature.

I have the honor to annex to this report a condensed statement,

which will serve to show the contents of a work I propose to publish, and which will contain a full account of what I personally
observed and inspected in Europe, with extracts from foreign
works, reports of committees, eminent writers, practical vintners,
farmers, horticulturists, manufacturers.

As soon as this work is completed, which will be, I think, before the adjournment of the Legislature, I will furnish a printed
copy to each branch of your honorable body.

Not having been able, since my recent return, to learn any thing
of my colleagues and their labors, I respectfully submit this as
my report, and I have the honor to be, with distinguished respect,
your obedient servant,

A. HARASZTHY,

Commissioner on the Improvement and Growth of the
Grape-vine in California.

CONTENTS.

CHAPTER V.

GERMANY, THROUGH SWITZERLAND, TO ITALY.

CHAPTER VI.

ITALY :—WINE AND SILK.

CHAPTER VII.

THE BORDEAUX WINE DISTRICT.

CHAPTER VIII.

JOURNEY THROUGH SPAIN: WINE, RAISINS, AND OLIVES.

CHAPTER IX.

GRAPES AND WINES IN CALIFORNIA.

GRAPE CULTURE,

WINES, AND WINE-MAKING.

GRAPE CULTURE AND WINE-MAKING.

CHAPTER I.

FROM SAN FRANCISCO TO PARIS.

Appointment as Commissioner.—Preparations.—Departure from California.—Circular Letter from Mr. Seward.—Voyage to Europe.—Arrival at Paris.—My Son.—Correspondence.—Departure for Dijon.

HAVING received from his Excellency the Governor, J. G. Downey, the appointment of "Commissioner upon the Ways and Means best adapted to promote the Improvement and Growth of the Grape-vine in California," I proceeded to Sacramento to lay my plan before the Governor, and received his sanction to go to Europe for the purpose of collecting information, and such vines and trees as in my judgment were best adapted for our State. The Legislature not having made any appropriation for the purpose of defraying the necessary expenses, I had to make use of my own means, which I cheerfully did, having been assured that my traveling expenses and money laid out for the purchase of the vines and trees would be refunded by the next Legislature. The Press in various parts of the State approved the mission, and spoke in favorable terms of the same; in fact, the general sentiment of the people favored and encouraged me in the undertaking.

Accordingly, I soon made my preparations, and on the 10th day of June, 1861, I started from San Francisco on the steamer *Golden Age*. The passage was pleasant and quick. Arriving in New York on the 4th of July, I rested for two days. I then proceeded to Washington to procure my passport. I was presented by Messrs. Latham and M'Dougal, United States Senators from California, to the Honorable William H. Seward, Secretary of State, who gave me a circular letter to the United States diplomatic agents in Europe, which reads as follows:

3

"To the Diplomatic Agents and Consuls of the United States in Foreign Countries.

"*Department of State, Washington, 6th July,* 1861.

" GENTLEMEN,—Mr. A. Haraszthy, the bearer of this communication, has been appointed by the government of the State of California to proceed abroad for the purpose of collecting information in regard to wine-producing countries, and reporting the results of his observations and inquiries to that government.

" I will consequently thank you to extend to him any facilities which may be necessary for so important an object.

" I am your obedient servant,
" WILLIAM H. SEWARD."

Having been furnished with the above letter and my passport, I returned to New York and embarked on the Hamburg steamer *Hammonia* for Southampton on the 13th of July. The passage was agreeable, the weather being fine. We arrived in port in the morning of July 26th.

After landing, we procured a carriage and drove into the surrounding country, examining several farms and manufactories. Returning to town in the evening, we took at midnight a French steamer for Havre, where we arrived next morning at 11 o'clock. The Custom-house officers very civilly passed our baggage without inspection. After partaking of a good breakfast at our hotel, we strolled through the town, and at 5 o'clock in the afternoon started in the extra train for Paris, where we arrived at 11½ o'clock that night.

We took lodgings in the Hotel de Louvre. The next day I saw my son Arpad, to whom I had telegraphed from Southampton. My son had been four years at school in Paris, and latterly in the Champagne districts, where he is now learning the manufacture of Champagne and other wines. He proved a great assistance to us during our stay in Europe; he acted as my secretary, my correspondence with scientific societies increasing daily, as well as with prominent officers of different governments. He copied also my journal entries, in which duty, however, he had the assistance of my daughter, as he was not able alone to copy both letters and journal.

The first day of our arrival being Sunday, we enjoyed a good rest, which was much needed after our long journey. The following day I called upon the United States minister, Mr. Dayton. This gentleman, being so much occupied in getting up his dispatches, was unable to receive me. Finding through his secretary that it would be several days before he would be able to see me, and it being doubtful whether he could aid me much in the way of introductions to presidents of horticultural and agricultural societies, I determined to write to them myself, inclosing a copy of my commission. This course was adopted for two reasons: first, because my own time was very limited, and, secondly, in order not to trouble the minister too much.

It was now the beginning of August, and every body who could do so was leaving Paris. We found the presidents gone with the rest to the country. We ascertained this fact several days after our letters had been written. Meantime we visited the vineyards and farms around Paris. Having ascertained the whereabouts of the officials, we started to Dijon, August 6th.

CHAPTER II.

THE BURGUNDY WINE DISTRICT.

August 6.—Left Paris for Dijon. The country through which
we passed was chiefly undulating hills planted with the sugar-
beet, which looked very fine. In the distance could be seen several sugar manufactories, with their tall chimneys and fine out-
buildings. All along the railroad the land was parceled out into
very small lots, eight or ten feet wide and two hundred feet long.
To one accustomed to the broad fields of America, it is very
strange to see so many strips of land, all belonging to different
persons. Of course, these lots are all planted according to the idea
of the owner; therefore, as you whirl rapidly by, you will see
first a patch of vineyard, then oats, wheat, barley, etc., creating a
very curious effect, till you know how valuable land is in this
densely-populated part of the world. On my way I also saw several fine meadows planted with clover, or what we Californians
call alphalfa. The strips of land are plowed in a curved shape
on the hill-sides and in very low land. The reason of this is, that
if the water were to run through a straight furrow it would be so
rapid that the soil would be washed away. The lands are from
four, five, to six feet, and thrown up by the plow, but it is done
most beautifully regular. I have seen several men plowing very

finely in spite of their plow, which is a primitive machine for this enlightened age. It is furnished with a wheel on the side of the beam.

Grain is now ripe, and they are beginning to harvest it. Men, women, and children may be seen in the fields, with sickles, hard at work. This is very singular to the eyes of a California farmer who finds the Reaper a slow machine which cuts from sixteen to twenty acres in the day, and requires binding, heading, and stacking; therefore he lays it aside for the Header, which cuts, thrashes, and bags his grain all in the same day. However, this machine could not be used in this part of Europe, where the land is subdivided into so many parcels, and the owners have enough help to pick the head off every stem, if it is necessary, with the hand; and, if a head should fall from the wagon, it is picked up with all care; so you may guess there is not much chance for herds of cattle in this part of France.

The grain does not grow to a great height here. The barley and oats are about eighteen inches or two feet, and the rye about two and a half feet high. On this route I did not see any wheat. For carrying the grain the inhabitants generally use a donkey. They pack on him the grain, straw, etc., whatever it may be. The wealthier class use a two-wheeled cart, which has a rack on both sides; in front and rear there is a fork, which resembles the fingers of an American cradle. To this is attached a rope, by which the rack may be lowered or raised. In this manner the cart is easily and well packed. Those who are too poor to keep a donkey carry the scanty produce upon their backs to their homes, which generally are four or five miles distant. From this the reader can well imagine that not even a blade of grass is allowed to be wasted.

The color of the ground in some places is white, but in general is a pale red, and very much exhausted. There are but few fruit-trees, and they are very badly attended to: they look very wretched. The vines are very small, and in the vineyards may be seen many yellow sprouts, which is a sign of decay.

We crossed several roads, all of which excited my greatest admiration by the fine order in which they are kept. They are smooth and hard as a billiard-table. All along their borders, at a distance of twenty yards, are piled up fine small stones: in case a hole should be made in the road, the inspector need only take a handful or two of these stones to fill it up immediately. This prevents it from becoming dangerously large; and both man and beast may travel all over France with perfect security and with pleasure. The meadows are generally shaded by poplars, planted in rows. The banks of the river and canal are also ornamented in the same manner, which has a very pleasing effect on the eye. We passed through many small villages, where there are some very ancient cottages built of gray stone, or still having the thatched roof. In the distance can be generally seen some château, peeping from beneath innumerable shade-trees.

The town where the train stops has several sugar manufactories surrounding it. After leaving this town the country begins to be hilly. The strata on the soil is lime and a mixture of magnesia cement. The whole is planted with vines, even the steepest hills, which a person ascends with difficulty. The vines here also show very yellow leaves and sprouts. Across the meadow, which is about two miles wide, on the left side of the road, the ground rises again into hills, all of which are planted with vines.

During our journey we passed through several tunnels of different lengths, but the last, about twenty miles from Dijon, was at least five or six miles long.

At six o'clock we arrived in Dijon; went to the Hotel de la Cloche, where, after washing off the dust that almost buried us, we took dinner at the table d'hôte. It was the finest dinner I have eaten since the beginning of my tour. There were more than a dozen dishes neatly served up and delicately cooked. After dinner we went out to look at the city. Walking through its principal streets we saw the City Hall, which is a fine, ancient stone building. The Cathedral, a time-honored edifice, with finely-proportioned columns and many Bible scenes carved in stone, may also be seen.

After taking a cup of coffee we returned home and addressed a letter to Professor Ladrey, and inclosed the letter I received to him from the editor of l'Echo du Pacific. I requested the favor of a personal interview. After dispatching this letter we retired, well satisfied with the city, dinner, and excellent bed.

I arose at seven o'clock, after passing a sleepless night. The whistle of the night-trains, the rolling of the omnibuses to and from the stations, kept me awake the whole night; and in the morning the chattering of men and women, the notes of a musical donkey immediately under my window, the shrill voice of the venders of fruits, vegetables, etc., deprived me of my morning's nap. After dressing we went through several of the squares or *rotondes* of the city (there are none of any regular form). There are to be found several fine fountains, and in the east half square a group of well-executed statues. There is a monk on the summit, supported by the figures of monks, popes, etc. The representation we could not make out. From these we went and inspected the interior of the Cathedral, the market, etc.

During our walk I saw several vines trained up to the second story windows of a house, and very heavily laden with grapes; a fair estimate would be seventy to eighty pounds to the vine. But what surprised me was that the grape-vine was planted so close to the house that the wall must rest upon half of its root, while on the other side are laid the heavy stones of the pavement, which must have rested there already many years. This is a positive proof that after a certain age a vine can live and bear a quantity of fruit without being hoed, or the ground loosened around its roots. These vines must be at least fifteen, twenty, or perhaps fifty years old. The leaves and fruit are large and healthy-looking. Upon pointing out the above to Arpad, he told me that a man named Rose had paved his vineyard as an experiment, but his successor, laughing at the idea, had the stones taken up, so that the experiment was never made. When I return home I will try it with vines of different ages. If it should succeed it would be a great economy, and the grapes resting on stone would be clean, and could not impart a ground taste to the wine from the quantity of dust which sometimes is upon them.

From these we went to the market. Here we found women sitting on both sides of the street selling fruit, vegetables, earthenware, etc. Leaving this noisy, and, I must confess, dirty-looking street, we turned into a covered market, where the women sell butter, cheese, etc. At the end of this market is a very large, ancient building, also filled with female venders of meats, fish, vegetables, etc. Here the noise reached its height, and resembled the hoarse roar of the Niagara Falls. Driven out by the old cheese and various other perfumes, we left to seek a more quiet and cleaner place.

I here found with astonishment that the fruit was inferior to that of California. The markets of San Francisco, Sacramento, Marysville, even the mining towns, produce a finer display of fruit than these large venerable towns. The reader must not suppose that I am influenced by partiality for my own State when I make my remarks. The object of my travels is especially to note down every thing in which the Europeans surpass us, and afterward lay them before the citizens of the United States. This task I will fulfill to the very best of my judgment.

At half past ten we returned to our breakfast, which did not prove inferior to our dinner of the preceding day. Indeed, it seems as though the landlords of Dijon are determined to fatten their guests at the shortest possible notice by administering to them the most delicate viands. The wine (which we added extra to our meal) was excellent. I say "added extra," because every guest is given a bottle of wine to his meal; and I will taste all the wines raised in the places through which I travel, as I wish to know whether the exported wines are worse or better than those which are common at home.

To-day Professor Ladrey called on us. During the conversation he promised to come in the evening, as, it being examination-day, he was occupied. He also offered his services for the next eight days to show us the surrounding vineyards, nurseries, orchards, etc. The professor is the editor of *La Bourgogne*, a monthly magazine on the culture of wine, and president of the Dijon wine district. He is also author of several chemical works on wine, etc. He seems to be a very gentlemanly and accommodating man. We met Monsieur Ladrey at seven. He spake very ably concerning the wine culture, and informed us that there was a fine botanical garden in the city. After leaving him we went through it, and also the old Cathedral, which boasts of a few fine oil paintings. There is also an aqueduct here worthy of notice; it extends four leagues from the city. By this means Dijon is well watered.

August 10.—This morning we went with Monsieur Ladrey through the botanical garden. The most interesting to me were the grapes, of which there are six hundred varieties. Partly planted at the foot of a high wall, they are trained over a net-like wire fastened to the wall. Some of these vines are twenty years old, and do not present a very inviting aspect, their leaves being withered, and mildew having attacked them and the grapes. The best and finest are the Persian Seedlers, which are transparent, with a beautiful healthy color, but a little late in the season. The Chasalas Fontainebleau looks thrifty and healthy, but the Palestine mammoth grape is poor, and most of the berries are dried up. The gardener ascribes this to the cold and changeable

weather they have had this year. The Catawba, Isabella, and
Scrapanay are among the varieties. The vineyard, placed on a
small gravelly knoll, is doing much better than the above-named
trellis-work. This may be on account of the vines not being so
old, as some are only two and six years old. On being told their
age, I was much surprised to see how small and feeble they were
in wood, and backward in bearing. I was told that they were
also manured. This is the first time many of them bear, as even
the acclimated vines do not produce fruit until they are five years
old, and very little then. After thanking the director, we agreed
to enter into correspondence, and exchange all varieties of vines,
seeds, etc., which the one does and the other does not possess.
This institution is supported by the city of Dijon. It does not
sell any of its roots, but exchanges with societies and individuals.

Upon leaving the garden we started for Gevrey, a small village half an hour's travel by railroad from Dijon, and which is
surrounded by the most celebrated vineyards in this district. As
the cars do not pass Gevrey, we stopped at Chambertin, took an
omnibus, and proceeded to Gevrey, having letters from M. Ladrey
to the overseer of a gentleman's vineyard. His absence from
home enabled us to take our breakfast before starting out. During the preparation of our meal, we endeavored to ascertain from
the talkative landlady whether a vehicle could be obtained. She
did not know; but her husband, upon our assuring him we were
not aristocratic, comforted us with the remote hope of procuring
us a coach to drive to some of the neighboring vineyards. We
were not able to get the promised conveyance till twelve o'clock.
Therefore we took a stroll through the village, which, like all
French towns, is irregular in its construction, and composed of
stone houses two stories high. The whole village has an air of
comfort and prosperity about it, which proves that even here the
cultivation of the vine is quite remunerative. At last our man
arrived. I put a series of questions to him, and gained the following information.

Gevrey is inhabited chiefly by peasants, either possessing vineyards in fee-simple, or renting for a period of time vineyards already planted, or warrant-lands which they have planted themselves. The rent of five acres of vacant land for planting a vineyard is 250 to 300 francs, payable annually, the term of the lease
being from 20 to 30 years. No allowance is made for the time
the vines are not bearing. Planted vineyards pay a rent of from

350 to 500 francs per five acres. The price of a vineyard, when for sale, varies with its location. The first class Pineau vineyards are worth from 40,000 to 60,000 francs per hectare;* the second class Pineau vineyards, 30,000 to 40,000 francs per hectare. The first class Gamai vineyards, 30,000 to 40,000 francs per hectare; the second class, 15,000 to 25,000 francs per hectare. The price of the wine is also very variable. For instance, wine raised in 1846 from a first class vineyard sold at 2000, 3000, and even 4000 francs per barrel, which contains 60 American gallons. In usual vintages, wine of the first class, when through the first fermentation, sells from 1000 to 1500 francs per barrel, sometimes even more; the second class, from 500 to 1000 francs. The wine made of the Gamai in celebrated years will sell for 800 to 1500 francs; in common years, 250 to 400 francs. Nearly all wines made here are red. The few white wines are not at all celebrated.

The mode of making the red wine is very much the same in the whole district. The grapes are picked by men, women, and children, from September to the 10th of October. They are placed in baskets, and carried to wooden tubs with leather straps on each side. There are several of them scattered in different parts of the vineyard. When these tubs are full, a man passes his arms through the straps, lifts the tub to his back, and carries it to the large trough which is placed in a central part of the vineyard. He empties the grapes into the trough, where the men crush them with their feet. The crushed grapes, juice and all, are then carried in a donkey-cart to the village, where they are thrown into a large fermenting-vat. The people do not live in their vineyards, but have their cellars generally in the village. The fermenting-vat is about 4½ feet high, and holds from 10 to 20 or even 30 barrels of wine. When they have remained in this tank from 24 to 40 hours, the fermentation will send the stems and seeds to the top of the vessel, forming a hard mass. Then, according to the size of the tank, from four to ten men, stripped of all their clothes, step into the vessel, and begin to tread down the floating mass, working it also with their hands. This operation is repeated several times, if the wine does not ferment rapidly enough. The reason given for this, in my eyes, rather dirty work, is that the bodily heat of the men aids the wine in its fermentation; but this object might be gained by throwing in heated stones, or using pipes filled with steam or hot water.

* The hectare is two and a half American acres.

After the above-named operation is completed, the wine is left to ferment two and a half to three and a half days longer, or four or five days from the time when the tank was filled. If the weather is warm, four days and nights are sufficient; if it is cold, it requires five days. In rare cases, the cellar is heated with stoves. The wine, after its fermentation, is drawn from the tank by a siphon, incased by a tube made of willows, with a wicker-work across the end, which is plunged through the seeds and stems to the bottom of the tank. If the end of the siphon was not covered by the wicker-work, it would soon be choked up by the stems and seeds. The clear juice flowing from the siphon is taken in tubs to the cellar, and emptied into barrels already in their places. These barrels are filled but two thirds full. When the tank has given up its clear juice, the stems, etc., are taken out, and put into a press, where the remainder of the juice is forced out. With this juice the barrels are filled to within two inches of the top. This wine remains quiet for about a month, when the barrel is completely filled and bunged up.

In the month of March these barrels are emptied into others, where the wine is cleared with eggs; then it is again drawn off in this first year of its existence. Many, in this district, draw off their wine as often as three times in the year. In years when the rains are heavy, or when from any cause the grapes are deficient in saccharine matter, sugar made from potatoes, known as " grape sugar," is added, to the amount, often, of thirty pounds to each sixty gallons. This is thrown into the vat where the wine is fermenting.

After a short conversation with the overseer, we were agreeably surprised to see a vehicle drive up to the gate. It was furnished with a good horse and driver, and was, moreover, a good example of the love of comfort cherished by the ancients, for that carriage has surely witnessed the rise and fall of many dynasties. Our landlord mounted the box with the overseer. The driver, on closing the door, asked our permission to place a lad of fifteen years in the box behind, where in good old times the servant took his place. Of course we had no objection, as it added to our aristocratic appearance, and the horse did not belong to us.

On leaving Gevrey, which is situated on rather high ground, we passed vineyard after vineyard, until we came to the elevation where are planted the Pineau grapes, which produce the celebrated red wines. The ground rises slowly to the top of the hill, and is of a red color, thickly strewn with gravel. The vines are planted two and two and a half feet apart, and not very regularly. The stems are not thicker than from three fourths to one and one and a half inches. The shoots are from three to three and a half feet high, where they are topped. They are tied to oak or locust sticks three and a half feet in height, and from one half to three fourths of an inch in thickness. The vines are tied either with straw or twigs. These vines, which we have imported, bear very small bunches, and also small berries. The clusters are more round than long in their form, and the berries are crowded so closely together that one overlies the other. The Pineau vineyards will give from eight to twelve barrels of wine to the hectare. This is generally a very productive year, but not a good wine season. The Pineau vines have only from one quarter to one and a half pounds of grapes; indeed, many vines did not have as much as a berry upon them.

We also examined the celebrated vineyards of Chambertin, the wine of which has a well-deserved and extensive reputation. At a short distance from there is a small village called Morey, which contains a fine cellar forty feet below the surface of the ground. It is all arched, is forty feet wide in the centre, and is supported by pillars of solid stone. The barrels are placed in three rows, two barrels high; but if the vault is much crowded, as many as four tiers are piled up. This cellar is furnished with four tanks, each capable of containing ten barrels of wine. These tanks have a door on the side, so as to enable a man to enter and clean the interior. To prevent leakage, the door is screwed tight to the side. Above this cellar there is still another one, arranged in the same way, which contains the young wines. We tasted many, and found them very good. Thence we went to the fermenting-room, where we saw the vats, press, tubs, etc., in excellent order. The fermenting-tanks, which hold from ten to eighteen barrels, are built of oak, with iron hoops to hold them together. The press, instead of having a screw from the top and pressing the juice out in that way, is made like a large square box, three sides of which are composed of thick wooden bars, about a quarter of an inch apart, so that the wine, but not the seeds and stems, may escape upon the large platform underneath the press, the bottom of which is also a lattice-work of strong bars. This platform is bordered by a scantling an inch and a half thick to prevent the juice from running over. The box above the platform is furnished with one solid oak slide, which is pushed toward the farther end by a couple of iron screws fastened in the planks on the one end. The other end has a cast-iron wheel, and each of the screws is furnished with one also, which in turn is driven by a still smaller wheel, on an iron bar which is attached to a fly-wheel worked by hand. When this is moved it starts the close-fitting solid slide of the box, and this presses the substance against the three open-work sides with such force as to extract every particle of juice from the stems and seeds deposited there for that purpose. The wine so pressed is carried in tubs to the cellar, and disposed of as before described.

Five days is generally sufficient for the fermenting of wine in this part, unless it is cold weather, when the overseer sends his men in a couple of times more in their costume *à l'Adam* to create the necessary warmth. The wine of this vineyard sells from 600 to 1500 francs, according to the excellency of the vintage.

We then went to examine the Gamai vineyards. We found that in color, size, and form the fruit very much resembled the Pineau grape; but the bunches are much larger, and the vines bear three times as much as the Pineau. I was told that a tract of land originally planted with the Pineau, which made an excellent wine, was replanted with the Gamai vine, which produced in this celebrated situation much less, and inferior wine to the vineyards of the first class Gamai in the plain. If this be a fact, it shows that the quality of wine depends greatly upon the grape, and *not* entirely on the soil. However, I will examine this theory more thoroughly, and compare it with the practical knowledge acquired by persons who have tried the same experiment.

After seeing every thing here, we returned to the village, discharged our driver, and took the cars for Dijon, where we arrived at six o'clock, very tired and hungry. However, we partook of white wine that evening, as the process through which the red wine goes did not serve to increase our longing for the ruby-colored liquid.

August 11.—This morning we started with M. Ladrey for Beaune, where the Professor L. is well acquainted. We were not very fortunate in our time, as it was Sunday, and almost every one was out. However, we at last found a clerk of a large commercial house which buys up the produce of the neighborhood. This gentleman took us into the vaults or cellars of his establishment. These cellars are the casemates of the ancient fortress which in olden times had its fortifications around the town. These casemates are now used by the inhabitants as wine-cellars. After descending a steep flight of steps about sixty feet below the surface of the earth, an immense vault met our aston-ished eyes. It was filled with barrels piled one upon the other. We were led from vault to vault, which now contain but 4000 barrels of wine, but they are capable of holding 12,000. There are also a few large hogsheads, which will hold forty-two bar-rels of wine. The thickness of these walls are forty feet. Of course, no private individual could build such a wall without its costing him a million of dollars. Little did the founders of this fort dream of the use to which their casemates would be put by the succeeding generations. The vaults in Beaune are now the best in the empire of France.

Having visited all the places of note, we stopped at a book-store and purchased the map of the surrounding vineyards, with the produce of the district marked; also two books of the dis-trict containing statistics of wine-making, the number of acres planted, their price, etc. After having freely conversed with the overseers who make a great deal of wine, I shall be able to judge whether the authors are theoretical or practical men. The maps are very valuable, as they give the quality of the vineyards as well as the nature of the soil.

We then started again for Dijon. The whole surrounding country is planted with vines—the hills with the Pineau, and the plains with the Gamai. Beaune is in the Prefecturate. It con-tains about 4000 inhabitants, who are generally wealthy and well to do. Much commerce is here carried on with foreign countries.

August 12.—This morning we took the cars for Clos Vougeot. We arrived there at noon, and immediately proceeded to the vine-yard of the Clos. The steward very kindly gave us all the de-sired information. He told me that those vineyards and houses formerly belonged to the priests, who, finding that the vine did well, planted the whole neighborhood. They also built the wine-presses which he now uses. These presses, four in number, were erected in the year 1117 A.D., and have defied the ravages of time. Their massive beams are sixty feet long, four and a half feet thick, and three feet wide, with a large wooden screw about eighteen inches thick and twelve feet high, still standing firm, and promising to last many years more.

There are in the press-house 36 tanks, containing 825 barrels, or 495,000 gallons of wine. The fermentation here lasts the same length of time as in other vineyards, namely, four or five days in warm weather, and six, or even twelve, in cold. When the weather is cold, the men are sent into the wine as often as three times in the day. As it is a most delicate operation to have the exact quantity of heat, the overseer informed me that he sometimes tested the wine three and four times in the day, either with a wine alcometer and thermometer, or with the palate. When the test is made with the alcometer, he takes portions from the different parts of the barrel—the top, centre, and bottom—and mixes them well together before testing.

We were also taken into the cellars, which are lined with hogsheads of 2400 gallons each. They are three and four hundred years old. They were also built by the priests, and are now kept in splendid order. The vineyards are planted with the Pineau and the Noirier half and half. The wine sells out of the fermenting-tub for 600 francs per barrel.

Burgundy wine was in ancient times considered the noblest and most generous of wines, except the Tokay; the wines from this district were often presented by the Princes of Burgundy to kings, princes, and chief nobles of foreign countries, as a great favor. No banquet was given without the genuine Burgundy; and even in the present age this fine wine holds its own with connoisseurs, and all lovers of a good glass. Industry and science have in modern times elevated the Bordeaux, and have made it a wine more generally used, on account of its mildness, as a table wine; but, nevertheless, the Burgundy is sought for by all nations, and the extensive district planted with its vines can not supply the wants of the trade.

That portion of the district which produces the finest wines is called the Côte d'Or, "Golden Hills." This is a range of hills from Chalons sur Saone to Dijon, running from north-northeast to south-southwest, about eighty miles in length. The height of these hills is from two hundred to three hundred feet; the soil is red and gravelly, containing a good deal of limestone, similar to our Sonoma soil, which also exists in almost every county in California by millions of acres. These hills, with the exception of small spots where the red rock comes to the surface, are planted with vines, the vineyards reaching almost to the top of the hills. The reason why they do not extend to the very crest is that no soil exists on the rocks toward the very top. The first quality of the wine is produced on the heights. The redder the soil, the better the wine.

I have mentioned that I visited the celebrated vineyard of Clos Vougeot, containing one hundred and eighty acres, surrounded with a solid stone wall. In the middle stands the ancient abbey, which once had more than one hundred monasteries tributary to it. It is a well-preserved edifice, and is now owned by a private family who spend a portion of the time on this domain.

The first-class vineyards plant exclusively the Pineau grape-vines, a black grape with a small berry and a small bunch, which produces from a half to one and a half pounds to the vine. This gives the generous and widely famed Burgundy wine.

The second-class vineyards contain the Gamai grape, black in color, considerably larger as to berries than the Pineau, and more prolific, but giving an inferior wine.

The third class are at the foot of the hills, sometimes extending into the valleys. They are planted with Gamai and several other vines, producing blue and white grapes.

The various experiments made with the fresh-pressed juice from the Pineau showed ninety-six degrees of sugar and the greatest weight; while the Gamai, raised alongside, proved to be only eighty-four degrees. In this province, when a vineyard is planted anew, the work is as follows: The ground is laid out with ditches five feet apart and one and a half feet deep; the ground is thrown between the ditches, making a ridge; the ditches are partially filled with good ground manure; the cuttings, eighteen inches long, are placed half a foot apart, bending toward the ridge; the soil is then drawn over the cutting and trampled down by the feet, leaving two buds out. The ridge is planted with potatoes, beans, beets, or cabbages. The first and second year, during the summer, these vines receive two or three hoeings. The first year these plantations do not receive any pruning, but are left to grow as bushy as nature will allow. The second year, in the spring, they are pruned to two buds, and more soil is drawn over, covering the plants up to the cut. Manure is also applied in the rows. In the third year the vines are pruned to two branches, each cut to two buds, and furnished with a stake from four to five feet long. During the fourth, or sometimes during the fifth year, small ditches are made from the vines toward the middle of the rows. The vine then is drawn in this ditch, the root remaining, with one branch, in its original place. The other branch is bent to the centre of the row, and two buds are left out of ground. The ridges which existed between the rows become, by this operation, leveled, and the whole vineyard now stands planted, two and a quarter feet apart, with vines. During the summer but one vine is allowed to grow up; all the other sprouts are rubbed off.

Many experiments were made by digging up the ground two feet deep, then taking an iron bar, and making a hole, and planting the cutting. This mode succeeded as well as that just described; that is, the vines grew and flourished well; but it was found that, after a certain number of years, the vineyards thus planted yielded but little; so that this mode is now abandoned, and the old ditching and laying system is now in use.

When the vines begin bearing, which is the fifth and sixth year, each retains but one stem, which is cut above the ground to three buds. This mode of cutting to three buds is repeated every year; that is, year after year the wood which possessed the three buds is left, and the new-made wood is cut to three buds. Proceeding thus, in from eight to ten years the vine will be raised to the height of from two to three feet. It becomes, therefore, necessary to bring these vines nearer to the ground, and by this means to renovate and rejuvenate them. This may be done in the following manner: As soon as the vintner sees that a vine is growing too high, he will, in the month of February or March, dig a ditch a foot deep and six inches wide toward a vacant place, without any reference to the line. The vine now is uncovered from the dirt on all sides, and drawn into this ditch. The hole (or ditch) must be just as long as the *old* stem of the vine, so that when laid horizontally the old stem will reach the end. The yearling branch at the end of the old stem is then bent up, the ditch filled with manured soil, and the yearling branch cut to three buds above the ground. About one tenth of the vines are annually so laid, consequently every vineyard is renewed once in ten years. By this operation, of course, all lines are destroyed, the vines standing every way like beans sowed broadcast; but, inasmuch as cultivation is carried on entirely by hand, it creates no inconvenience.

The vineyards are generally divided into *ouvries* (land of a day's work). Such an ouvrie is 3645 square feet, in which ten to fifteen vines are to be laid every year by the hired vintner as a part of his regular duty, the payment being included in his wages; but if it should exceed the above number of vines, he is paid one

D

sou for each extra vine. The usual wages for working an acre for the year, excepting the packing of the grapes and making the wine, is from eighty to a hundred francs per acre. Many proprietors give their lands on half shares, as I have already mentioned.

The practice of manuring the vines is a necessary evil. It is a well-understood fact that vines produced on soil not manured will be more durable, and clear better, and are, consequently, sooner ready for market.

The general conviction in this district is, that the closer the bud to the main stem, the stronger the wine it will produce; that is, the first bud from the old wood will give grapes less in size than the second and third buds, but it will be a better wine. It is also demonstrated that the top bud will produce wood which is much more prolific in bearing than the wood of either of the other buds.

The reader will understand that by cutting the vine to three buds it will make, of course, three branch vines. The sprouts must be rubbed off, so that these three vines will grow vigorously, and enable the grapes to grow to perfection.

It is generally admitted by all the vintners and French writers that, the closer the vines are kept to the ground, the better the grapes will ripen, and they will contain more saccharine and coloring matter. It is also agreed unanimously by all reports on this subject, that when vines are pruned for large crops many buds will be left on the vines, which will produce many grapes, but they will be neither as sweet nor as dark colored as the grapes from the moderate-bearing vines, besides making an inferior wine without the proper bouquet. In the district of Burgundy the practice of three-bud pruning is in general use. The vineyards being renewed every ten years, as described above, are, of course, kept in splendid condition. We were told that the Burgundy vines exported to foreign countries, and not cultivated in the manner above described, in fifteen or twenty years ceases to bear entirely, or, if at all, in very small quantities.

The vintage is conducted as follows: Those proprietors of vineyards which have stone walls around them, called "*des Clos*," are allowed to gather their grapes whenever they please; consequently, they will begin the vintage whenever their grapes are in the very best condition. This accounts for the fact that the wine from fenced vineyards is better in quality, and commands a higher price in the wine market than that of others.

Those vineyards not fenced, and the largest portion, are subject to the following rules: Three commissioners on vineyards—one proprietor, one merchant, and one vintner—are appointed by the préfect, for the purpose of examining the vineyards from time to time, and reporting to the sub-préfect. When in their judgment the vineyards are fit for the vintage to begin, they report the fact. At the receipt of this report, the sub-préfect issues his order, setting the day recommended by the commissioners for the work to begin. On this day every body is compelled to commence the vintage; but, as their work is performed in a few days, the custom is to order a certain day in one village; in an adjacent one a few days later, and so on, so that sufficient hands can be procured to perform the necessary labor. If this were not done in districts where several hundred thousands of acres are planted with vines, it would be impossible to get the labor necessary, all at the required time.

The laboring men, women, and children, at such appointed time, come from far and near, and collect at the market-place; here they are hired by the vintners, according as they are needed. They are paid more or less, according as the number of laborers are greater or fewer. The gathering is described elsewhere.

The possessors of small vineyards usually sell their grapes to wine-dealers, who come to the vineyards. They either purchase by the measure, or take the whole produce of the vineyard in a lump. The owner of the vineyard invariably has to gather and deliver the grapes to the purchaser, and to pick and select them according to the desire of the merchant.

Those proprietors who have but small vineyards, and do not sell their grapes, but make them into wine, produce, without exception, an inferior quality; not on account of the locality or soil, but for the reason that they do not or can not select their grapes, but throw all together, good and bad—the amount of grapes being too small to make different qualities of wine; the consequence is, that their wine brings indifferent prices.

It is believed, and we think with good reason, that the fewer the grapes on the vine the more perfect they will be, and will receive from nature the full aroma natural to the species, and which makes the wine so celebrated for its bouquet.

Having examined the district of Burgundy in every direction, collecting all useful information, and engaging several thousand cuttings of its celebrated varieties, we prepared to return to Paris.

But, before leaving Dijon, I must here acknowledge my heartfelt thanks to Professor M. Ç. Ladrey for the kind attention we received at his hands, and for the valuable information, books, reports, etc., which he presented to me. To his accomplished lady and family our gratitude likewise is due. We had the pleasure of partaking of a magnificent entertainment with them.

After bidding farewell to our new acquaintances, we started at midnight by the train for Paris. As it was night we could see nothing, so that we had to spend the time as best we could.

CHAPTER III.

FROM PARIS TO FRANKFORT ON THE MAINE.

Ball at the Chateau des Fleurs.—The Emperor's Fête-day.—The Illumination and Fireworks.—Orderly Conduct of the People.—Departure for Germany.—Observations on the Way.—Ems.—The Casino.—Gambling.—The Promenade.—Dr. Precht.—Donkey and Mule Riding.—The Valley of the Swiss.—Count Stein's Tomb.—Grist-mills.—The Water-wheels.—Silver Mines.—Condition of the People.—The Theatre.—Letters and Visits.—Coblentz.—Difficulty with Bankers.—Start for Frankfort.—Letters of Credit preferable to Cash.—Conversation with Passengers.—Notes by the Way.—Arrival at Frankfort.—Letters of Introduction.—Americans in Frankfort.

August 14.—Arrived in Paris at six o'clock in the morning, after having traveled almost the whole night. I was busily engaged the whole day in writing answers to my correspondents. In the evening, hearing that a public ball was to be given at the Chateau des Fleurs, I determined to see what such a thing was in Paris. The ball was given in the open air, in a garden most beautifully illuminated with lamps of all colors and descriptions. Some were shaped like flowers, and, as such, were scattered profusely among the shrubbery; others represented garlands, and were festooned among the trees, creating a perfect blaze of light. Then there were gas-lights nestling in among the flowers, glittering like so many dew-drops. At the farther end of the avenue was a fine pagoda for the music; this was also most brilliantly illuminated. The whole, when viewed from an elevated platform, had a most entrancingly beautiful effect. But the company was not such as we would like our families to associate with. Most of the females were *grisettes*, each of whom, at the tones of the inspiring band, seemed to forget for the moment her cares and troubles, and to have but one idea—that of excelling her rivals in the dance. After gazing for a time upon this scene of wild gayety, I returned home much fatigued.

August 15.—To-day I intended to leave Paris; but as it is the Emperor's fête-day, and there will be grand illuminations in the city, I have determined to remain over one day.

Evening has arrived. Carriages have been forbidden to go to

the Champs Elysées; the Rue de Rivoli leading to it is in a blaze. Millions and millions of lights decorate public and private houses. The garden of the Tuileries has been transformed into fairy-land. Sceptres and crowns, blazing with lights to represent the finest rubies, diamonds, topazes, and emeralds, are scattered all over. Down the main avenue may be seen, at a distance of every ten or twelve feet, immense chandeliers of wire supporting hundreds of lights. The ponds are encircled with lamps. From the Tuileries we could see the principal public buildings, all of which were encircled with a double row of small gas-lights, which resembled a crown of brilliants. All the columns were wound around with lamps of all sizes and colors. Among the numerous designs was that of the Legion of Honor. It was elevated above the house-top, and the imitation of precious stones of which it is composed was elegant. The River Seine was also festooned all along with garlands upon garlands of lamps. In the Champs Elysées was a square, containing four Chinese towers, composed of different-colored lamps. Circle was within a circle, till you thought you could see almost into futurity. These four pagodas were connected with triple garlands of lamps of all colors, caught up at equal distances by bunches of lamps of different forms. The Invalides, however, was the most beautiful, but it requires a more skillful pen than mine to give a description of the decorations. Near the Invalides were also the fireworks, which were magnificent. Fountains, rockets, wheels—in a word, every thing that art could produce in that line, was there exhibited that evening. As for the spectators, there must have been at least one million present. Men, women, and children all thronged to see the fireworks, and for hours the principal street was nothing but a sea of heads.

There were guards and policemen placed at different points, and, notwithstanding this almost incredible number of people, there were no fights, no picking of pockets, no disturbance. All was quiet and well arranged. Every one seemed to enjoy the sight, without having before his eyes the continual fear of being robbed. The free approval and calm behavior of the people showed that they are accustomed to such grand sights. What struck me as strange was, that the Emperor was not in Paris at this grand celebration, but remained at his country seat at St. Cloud.

August 16.—This evening at five o'clock we left Paris for Coblentz. Daylight lasted but three and a half hours, so I saw but few of the villages through which we passed. There are many stone-quarries on the way between Coblentz and Paris. From these quarries the stone is transported to Paris either by rail, river, or canal.

In this district the soil is much richer than in Dijon, but the wine is not celebrated, as the ground is entirely planted with grain, and the laborers raise only enough grapes for their own use.

I noticed that a great deal of hemp is cultivated in this part. It looks very well, as also do the clover-fields, which one and all are in splendid condition. Poplar-trees are planted in great profusion, and afford a fine shade. The grape-vines on the hill-sides looked very luxuriant, and were devoid of the red spots which I noticed in the districts of Dijon and Beaune. We went too rapidly to judge as to the quality of the crop.

We passed village after village till dark, when we composed ourselves quietly for a nap, but an undisturbed slumber was not attained. No sooner had I fixed myself comfortably, and was already in my first doze, when a stentorian voice demanded " *les billets.*" Arousing myself with difficulty, I fumbled in every pocket, until, by chance, I reached the right one which contained the tickets, which the conductor glanced at and returned. This process was renewed every hour, till finally I was worked up almost to desperation. But fortunately this, as all troubles, had an end, and we reached Cologne, where we changed cars for Coblentz. I forgot to say that, upon reaching the Prussian borders, we were hustled out into the Custom-house, where we were very civilly treated by the officers, only going through a pretense of examination.

August 18.—I took a carriage, and went to Ems with my family. The road leading there winds along the banks of the river, and is at the foot of the mountains, which are all planted with vines; but the whole mountain being nothing but slate, every few rods there are high rock walls which form a sort of platform, and on these are planted vines, which look well, but the wine is inferior, as the soil is slate-rock and sand. We passed several large iron factories on the road to Ems, where we arrived at half past nine o'clock.

Ems is the property of the Duke of Nassau, and yields him an annual income of two millions of dollars. Every thing is very finely arranged, and not costly for a bathing-place.

We took a promenade after dinner, and passed into the Casino, where there are two large gaming - tables, around which were crowded numerous spectators and betters, among whom I observed several ladies, throwing down their coins on the red or black. I was told that, a short time since, a count lost all he had and blew his brains out, while a more lucky individual broke the bank and won 52,000 thalers. But I soon left, as I did not expect to be lucky like the latter, nor want to fare like the former.

August 19.—A beautiful strain of music awoke me from a most pleasant sleep to a most beautiful morning. The band, composed of forty musicians, paid by the Duke, plays every morning from six to eight o'clock. Hastily putting on my clothes, I went upon the promenade, which was crowded with genuine patients, and pretty patients who wished to attract attention by their apparently delicate health, but in reality showed themselves to make a good match. I was much amused by the various manœuvres of the mammas, who were on the *qui vive* not to let their inexperienced daughters make a blunder.

The day was passed in visiting the grounds and neighborhood, and in forming acquaintances. We met here our sincere and good old friend, Dr. Precht, with whom an appointment had previously been arranged by telegraph. He was accompanied by his lady. Our meeting proved a mutual gratification. After partaking of a good dinner, accompanied by a few bottles of the best wine the cellar of the Duke could furnish, we passed the remainder of that day admiring the beautiful promenades, rapt sometimes in the enticing charms of music, or beholding with admiration the loveliest beauties of all nations who gather here.

August 20.—In the morning, at six o'clock, we were all up to take a donkey-ride and see the surrounding country. The custom here is to ride donkeys. Those destined for ladies have on them a kind of arm-chair saddle, well wadded, open on one side, and with a back on the other. The color of the cover is a gay red, and the whole concern is very convenient. This is placed on a small donkey, hardly larger than a Newfoundland dog, who trots off with his burden with the greatest seeming ease. The ladies were delighted with their long-eared chargers and their easy gait.

Each donkey has a driver, who remains close behind the animal to quicken its speed or guide it. This latter operation is done by twisting the donkey's tail to the right or to the left, just as he is wished to go. Our party was composed of three ladies, myself, and Arpad. We men rode mules, which, in my estimation, were not as good as the donkeys, inasmuch as these, with the ladies, were always ahead of us, and it was only with the continual exertion of our heels and the application of the driver's stick that we could catch up with them.

Our drive was toward a valley called the "Valley of the Swiss." The road ascends to the top of a well-timbered mountain, and then descends into the above-mentioned valley. On the side of the hill, before descending into the Swiss valley, is the family vault of Count Stein, minister of the King of Prussia, and a celebrity of the time of Napoleon the First. This vault, which also holds several members of the family, is of stone, and is a building of simple construction. It is surrounded by a small garden containing several pine-trees, and which itself is encircled by a stone wall. A woman came and opened, first, the gate of the wall, and then the iron door of the vault. After we had seen all that was to be seen, which was a couple of sculptures and as many inscriptions, we left the resting-place of the dead, and wound our way down the narrow path into the valley.

The path was so steep and so narrow that we were obliged to dismount and descend on foot. On our way down we passed several small grist-mills, whose working force was given by a small stream. The water runs along in a ditch, and is brought in a wooden trough, one foot wide and about six inches deep, over a bucket-wheel. I examined one of these wheels: it was twenty-eight feet high and one foot wide; its bucket holds about a gallon and a half of water. The water running was but one and a half inch deep and twelve inches wide. The stones and inside arrangements are all very primitive. As for the construction of the wheel, round the axle is built a cog-wheel, the cogs being on the side, and turning a small spindle with seven horizontal rods, this spindle, in its turn, turning the stone. Much improvement might be made in the stone and all the other arrangements. I was informed by the miller that he makes about ten bushels a day. The flour is bad, and would not be marketable with us.

We passed several silver mines; they are being worked with good advantage to the proprietors. I intend to visit at least one of the smelting establishments. Perhaps they contain some new improvements by which Washoe might derive some benefit.

We at last arrived home, much pleased with our donkey-ride,

but less so with the information which I gathered; the land is poor, the people poor; the mountains are not even fit for the vine culture. The country gives but meager earnings to its inhabitants, and, were it not for this bathing-place, they would fare still worse. Ems brings together thousands of people each year from far and near, either for pleasure or to partake of its mineral waters, whose healing virtues have a wide reputation. The tax on agricultural lands in the Duchy of Nassau is six dollars on the thousand. Mechanics pay a much larger tax.

We went this evening to the theatre. The acting was pretty good. There was present a fine array of ladies. The diamonds sparkled, the pearls, rubies, etc., rivalized with each other, but the captivating eyes of the ladies were above all the diamonds and pearls.

August 21.—Long before the beautiful band of music began to play I was up writing letters to my correspondents in Europe, and then continued my journal. Having not much to write from the doings of yesterday, I finished in the forenoon, and then received several visits. Having been invited to dine with Dr. Precht, myself and family went to dinner. During the day I sent some letters and papers to Count Wass, also to Mr. Grisza. In the evening I received Mr. Ordödy, a Hungarian nobleman, and his lady. During the evening we received several other visits, after which we went for an hour to the ball. Returning from the ball, I read some books on wine and wine-growing, after which I prepared for my departure to the upper parts of the Rhine.

August 22.—I started in the morning for Coblentz with Dr. Precht and Arpad. Arrived in Coblentz, I called on the banker to whom I had a letter of credit, but, to my surprise, he informed me that he had received no notice from Hentsch and Lutscher, consequently he could not pay me any money on my letter of credit. What was to be done? I had but three florins in my pocket, and a bill for five days' living for myself and family in Ems. I at once telegraphed to Frankfort, where the same letter of credit was addressed to another banking-house. From this house I received the answer that they had been notified from Paris, and so I at once started for Frankfort.

From Coblentz to Frankfort by railroad it takes five hours fifteen minutes, and the fare in the second class is two and a half thalers per seat. In Germany only the nobility and higher classes, or, to use a colloquial term, the *Big-bugs*, travel in the first class. The railway carried us past many celebrated vineyards; but, as the money was at *low tide* in our pockets, we were forced to delay our investigations till high tide, which we hoped would take place, as usual, in twenty-four hours or less.

This money affair would have been more annoying than it really was had it not been for Dr. Precht, who furnished me with twenty-five florins to proceed on my way to Frankfort. It was altogether brought on by the carelessness of the corresponding clerk of the house Hentsch and Lutscher. I purposely put this little accident in my report to warn my fellow-citizens who travel never to let their purse run down low enough to prevent themselves from reaching the next-named place on their letter of credit. A letter of credit, in traveling, is preferable to cash, as this may be lost or be stolen; besides, the constant change of money in the different countries constitutes a certain loss, not taking into consideration that *changers* are never over-honest people. Not only, then, is a letter of credit safer, but also much more preferable.

On the road from Coblentz I opened a conversation with a clergyman, who gave me some information on vines and their varieties. I also had a conversation with the proprietor of a vineyard, who is himself manufacturing wine. He recommends to me in very high terms the hydraulic press, to press out the juice from the pulp of the grapes. He added that this new press, only introduced five years ago, works admirably well, and that all those who make any progress in wine manufacturing introduce it into their establishments. I asked him why they had abandoned the cylinder crushers, and again adopted the old method of stamping with the feet or with wooden pieces? I was answered that cylinders crush more or less of the stems, which, containing a bitter juice, communicates the flavor to the wine, destroying some of its bouquet, and making it less palatable. In regard to nurseries, the general answer I receive is, that there are none of any consequence in the neighborhood. The trees on the road have no fruit at all. Some attribute this to the frost, others again to the last year's crop, which was extraordinarily heavy, and consequently spoiled this year's. I told them that in America we had a mode of regulating, to some extent, the bearing of our trees by root-pruning them. They listened attentively, but I saw by their smiles, which were hardly suppressed, that they very much doubted my statements. The people here, in general agricultural knowledge, are much behind ours of the same class. We arrived in

Frankfort at half past ten in the night, where we took a beef-steak, and then went to bed.

August 23.—I, as usual, wrote my journal in the morning. After nine o'clock I went with Arpad to my banker Metzler, who paid me the required money, and kindly offered me his services and letters of introduction to several proprietors of large vine-yards—among others, one at Johannisberg. I accepted his offers with thanks.

From here we went to the American consul general, Mr. Rick-er. Inquiring about Mr. Ross Browne, I found that he was ab-sent, traveling in Norway, but was expected back daily. From the consul's we went and took a walk around the city for half an hour, then returned to the hotel to write our correspondence, etc. We were not long thus occupied before Mr. Howard, son of General Volney Howard, of San Francisco, called upon us. This young man is studying medicine in Europe. I invited him to dine, and after dinner he went with us to *Hochheim* by railroad.

CHAPTER IV.

HOCHHEIM, STEINBERG, AND JOHANNISBERG.

Hochheim.—Mr. Dresel.—The Champagne Manufactory.—Mr. Lembach.—His
Cellar.—His Method of Wine-making.—Different Wines from the same Grape.—
The Barrels.—Sulphuring the Barrels.—Price of Wines.—Regulations for Gather-
ing the Grapes.—Visit to the Champagne Manufactory.—Mr. Hummel.—Wies-
baden.—Professor Medicus.—The Kurhaus.—The Gambling Rooms.—Dr. Thomä.
—Biberich.—The Chief of the Steinberg Vineyards.—The Steinberg Vineyards.
—Mode of Cultivating the Grape.—The Farm-yard.—Eberbach.—The Wine
Cellars.—Tasting Wines.—Bouquet of Old and New Wines.—How to taste fine
Wines.—Assorting the Grapes.—Manufacturing the Wine.—Large and small
Barrels.—Requisites for making good Wines.—The Presses.—Visit to Johannis-
berg.—The Soil of the Region.—Vineyards not Sold.—Their Value.—Palace of
Johannisberg.—The Vineyard.—The Cellars.—The Johannisberg and Steinberg
Wines.—Rivalry between them.—The Superiority sometimes accidental.—A
lucky Stroke.—Prices the same.—Last Glasses of Johannisberg.—Geisberg.—
The Experimental Gardens.—Results of Experiments.—High Trimming and low
Trimming of Vines.—The School of Agriculture.—Exchange of Seeds.—Depart-
ure for Frankfort.—Report of Wine Auctions at Eberbach.

In an hour's travel we arrived at Hochheim, where, after going
to an inn and having our clothes brushed, we set out to see Her-
man Dresel, Esq., Director of the Champagne manufactory of the
Joint-stock Association.   The American consul had furnished me
with a letter of introduction to Mr. Dresel.   He received me
kindly, and conducted us through the whole establishment, to describe which, at first sight, would be impossible.   This is one of the
largest establishments in Germany.   It employs eighty men, and
makes daily three thousand bottles of Champagne.   The capital
invested is 1,000,000 *güldens* (about $400,000).*   It makes very
good sparkling wines, and imitates excellently the French Champagnes.   Some of the imitations are really much better than the
brands they pretend to imitate.   The establishment makes money.
Mr. Dresel, who took great pains to show and explain to us each
branch separately, invited me to come to-morrow for a closer examination and farther inspection.   This gentleman is the brother
of Mr. E. Dresel, resident and proprietor of a fine vineyard in Sonoma.   I was ignorant of this until I asked the gentleman if he

* The *gülden* (plural *güldens*) or *florin* is equal to about 40 cents.

was not related to a Dresel in California. His answer that he was a brother only brought us closer together in our relations, and we conversed as old acquaintances. The cordial and gentlemanly manner of Mr. Dresel I shall not soon forget.

After spending a couple of hours in the establishment, and tasting some sparkling wine, we returned to our inn. Mr. Dresel joined us at our supper, and we spent an agreeable evening. In fact, we were up until half past eleven, which for a village is a pretty late hour. Parting with Mr. Dresel, with the promise of seeing each other next day for a thorough inspection, I went to bed well contented with to-day's travel and the result of the inspection. I was also contented with the wines we had drunk, for they were very good.

August 24.—After completing my journal of yesterday, we went to take a cup of coffee, then started out with our host, Mr. Lembach, who is a cooper as well as inn-keeper. He has the superintendence of several cellars belonging to persons who do not reside here. We went to a press-house, where we saw two presses with screws; one screw received its resisting point from below, the other from above. Neither of these presses are desirable for imitation.

From here he led us to his own wine-cellar, where he has about seventy *stück*, or pipes, each holding about two hundred and fifty gallons of wine. He gave us to taste wines of three successive years, coming from the same vineyard, forming eleven different wines. These wines were made purely from the Riesling grape; no other variety of grape was in them. The bouquet was fine; the wine clear and excellent. We tasted each wine separately, then compared one with the other. The difference from year to year was remarkable—so great that I was able to distinguish each year. He had first and second quality from the same wine. His mode of making wine is as follows: The grapes are gathered after the dew has dried up, and are carried to the press-house, where the bunches are separated into three, and in some celebrated vineyards into five classes. Each bunch of the first class is carefully divested of the rotten berries, dust, or other impurities. These classes, once formed, are worked separately and always kept apart. The grapes, once separated, are thrown into a crusher, where they run through two cast-iron cylinders. When once through this instrument they are put into a small vat, where they ferment six, eight, and even sixteen hours, but are carefully pressed down whenever the stems or seeds show themselves on the top.

This mode of fermenting for several hours is not adopted with blue grapes; it is only used for white grapes, and for making white wine from them.   To make white wine from blue grapes, you must not ferment them, for that will immediately color it.

The grapes, having fermented for the above-mentioned time, are put in a mass and pressed.   In a good year, that is, when the grapes are perfectly ripe and almost raisins, the second or last run makes the best wine.   When the grapes are not wholly ripe, the first run, or first pressed juice is thought to make the best wine. The reasons given for this are, that when the grapes are ripened to raisins they contain but little juice, and it is only extracted by a very powerful pressure, and this pressure only comes at the end; but when the grapes are full, and retain all their fluid, the first pressure gives the finest juice, as after it the pressure becomes greater and crushes the seeds and stems, which then discharge some of their bitter contents, which injures the wine.   In the first instance, when the grapes are almost raisins, the stones or seeds are also crushed, but they are dry, and are totally void of juice.

The juice is then run into barrels, in the cellar, of one stück (250 gallons) each.   These barrels, of course, are only in small vineyards, as in larger ones tuns, containing from two to five thousand gallons, are employed.   These vessels, large or small, once filled, remain for a time covered with a clean rag on the bung-hole.   They remain thus until March, when they are drawn off into clean barrels.   These barrels, if possible, are sulphured a day before being used.   If there is a deficiency of barrels, those must be employed which have already been used, but only after having been thoroughly washed and sulphured.   The first year the wine is drawn off into new barrels four or five times.   It is first drawn off four or five weeks after it is put into barrels, then in two months after, then in three, then in four.   In the second year twice will be sufficient; in the third year, once; then once in two years; and after that it may remain in the same barrel until it is bottled.   The greatest care should be taken never to leave a vacant space in any barrel holding wine.   As our host quaintly said, "You should sooner forget to kiss your wife on returning home than to leave a vacancy in your barrel."

When any barrels are empty, immediately wash them out thoroughly; for each barrel take a sulphur strip, one inch wide and four long, and burn it in the barrel; then bung it up well, and place it where it will be neither too dry nor too wet, as either extreme will injure it. Three months after, open the barrel, burn half as much as before, then bung it up, to begin again three months after. This is done on all the empty barrels. This operation serves to keep the barrel good and sweet. Should any acid or mould creep into the barrels, take a handful of quick-lime, put it in, pour hot water on it, and wash the barrel well. The price of a new barrel of 250 gallons is 40 *gildens* or florins ($16).

The cleanliness of all the wine-cellars in this country is admirable and most difficult to describe. The vineyards in good bearing years in Hochheim will produce one stück per *morgen* (somewhat less than an acre). The wine per stück sells at from 500 to 3000 florins ($200 to $1200). The wines are splendid, and really delightful to drink.

The authorities are so jealous of the reputation of their wine that no man is permitted to gather his grapes before the time for the vintage is decided by a council. To prevent imprudent men from plucking in the morning, when the dew is still on the grapes, it is forbidden to begin gathering before the large bell of the town has sounded. The same bell also sounds the hour of quitting the vineyard, when every one must cease to gather. Besides these regulations there are many others, as, for instance, a man planting a vineyard has to plant his vines three and a half feet apart, this being considered the best distance for the Riesling grape. Other varieties have different distances allowed to them; the Oestreicher, for instance, must be planted four feet apart, being a grape which produces more wood.

After having examined all the wines, and listened to much valuable information from our good host, we went to the manufactory of sparkling wines to see Mr. Dresel, with whom I had made an appointment. This time I made arrangements to procure all the varieties of vines grown in the neighborhood, and each kind of implement used in the manufacturing of sparkling wine. We once more went through all the cellars and warehouses, Mr. Dresel having introduced me to Mr. H. J. Hummel, superintendent of the wines and cellars. This young man has risen through all the branches of the art until he reached the position which he now occupies. He is a very intelligent man, and, as I am told, is a perfect master of his art. I spoke to him of coming to California to put up for me a similar establishment, if not so great in extent, at least producing as good wines. He promised to consider the matter, and, if the company gives its consent, he will do so. We spent no less than four full hours in this mammoth establishment, after which we returned to our inn, where Mr. Dresel soon rejoined us. After dinner we parted, Mr. Howard going to Frankfort, myself and Arpad to Wiesbaden, being furnished with several letters of introduction from Mr. Dresel.

We arrived at about five o'clock P.M., and immediately set out to see Professor Medicus, who is a professor in the government School of Agriculture for the education of youth in agricultural knowledge. The professor was absent from town, so we took a stroll in front of the *Kurhaus*, where a band of music was playing. The promenade was full of gay people. This bathing-place is larger than Ems, has splendid buildings, promenades, parks, fountains, etc. It also belongs to the Duke of Nassau, who resides here in winter. The waters are considered very good for curing several diseases.

Following a steady stream of people, we soon found ourselves in a splendid saloon, magnificently decorated, possessing no less than seven immense chandeliers hanging from different parts of the saloon, besides hundreds of other gay burners, all ornamented with ground glass globes. The richness of the furniture was in harmony with the rest of the decorations. The saloon has galleries where the music plays when balls and concerts are given. At the west end of the gallery and building there is a large place decorated with red velvet and gold trimmings for the use of the Duke and family.

In this vast saloon there is a gambling-table, surrounded by men and women, who are players or spectators. From here to the left open three more large saloons, also magnificently furnished and decorated. In the centre of each there is a gambling-table, occupied by players. At two tables they played at rouge et noir, and at the other two at roulette. These places are open to the public, and ladies and gentlemen come in for amusement to play or see the players. They seat themselves around in the rooms on arm-chairs or well-cushioned sofas. Liveried servants are in attendance. No smoking or loud talking is allowed, and hats must be removed from the head. From the last of the three gambling-rooms you enter into a fine large reading-room, where the prominent periodicals and newspapers published in Europe are to be found.

E

We spent a quarter of an hour in the last playing-room, where we watched a gentleman, who, with the greatest coolness, put up and lost from twenty to forty napoleons ($80 to $160) at a time. We at last went to our hotel, where, after supper, we went to bed.

August 25.—Being Sunday, nothing could be done in the morning except to send a letter to the director, Professor Dr. Thomä, chief of the Giesberg Agricultural Establishment, of which I have already made mention. At three o'clock I received an answer that the director would receive us at four. We accordingly went at that hour, and were received very cordially. After showing my commission, etc., the doctor kindly offered to conduct us to the Institute. He also said it would be better for us to go with him to Biberich, where the Duke is residing, and where also the chief of the wines and cellars is at present. Accordingly, we took a carriage and drove over to the Residence, which is about a mile and a half distant. Arriving there, we were presented to the chief, who was surrounded by gentlemen engaged in the agreeable occupation of drinking wine. The chief is an old gentleman over seventy-five years, unable to walk on account of the gout; still, he received us kindly, and readily gave me all the information I desired. He appointed that to-morrow I should go with his deputy (as he can not leave the house) to the different vineyards and cellars.

In the evening we returned from Biberich, but not before taking a walk in the gardens of the Residence of the Duke of Nassau. The Burg is of ancient architecture, large, standing on the banks of the Rhine, being surrounded on three sides by a fine park containing green-houses, exotics, etc. The trees are old and luxuriant. The town itself is built around the park. It has some fine buildings, but it does not equal Wiesbaden.

August 26.—As I was writing the above, the Director Thomä was announced. He came prepared to accompany me to the various places which the day would permit us to visit. I was much pleased at last to come to a place where the people are punctual, and ready to go to work at seven o'clock. We drove to Biberich. Here the old gentleman received us at the door of his receiving-room, having been assisted there by his valet. He put at our disposal his deputy. With him we proceeded to the celebrated vineyard of Steinberg. This vineyard disputes the superiority of the Johannisberg, and, of course, of the whole Rhine country. It contains 104 *morgen*. Its soil is rocky, and composed of a bluish clay, though the substrata is gravel. The vines are only Riesling; the distance at which they are planted is three feet in the rows, and four feet between the rows. The vineyards last about thirty years, when they are cut out, and the land rests for three years. During the first of these three years they haul some of the manured blue clay, and spread it over the vacant ground about a foot thick. This is done during the summer. Then it is plowed over several times, and clover raised upon it during its years of rest. The average yield of this vineyard is 40 stück, or 10,000 gallons.

Adjoining this vineyard is a farm-yard, which is leased for a period of time, with all the land, to a farmer; but he is obliged to furnish so many loads of manure annually, as it is indispensable to the Steinberg vineyards. I also saw his milk-house, and his cattle, which are not allowed to leave the stable even for watering. He considered his stock very fine, but I have seen much better in California.

From there we went to the old Convent of Eberbach, which is at present partly a state Penitentiary, and the remainder is the cellar of the Duke of Nassau. The deputy master of the cellars opened them, the coopers belonging to the cellars entered, and in about a quarter of an hour we were invited to go in. Upon coming into the cellar a beautiful sight lay before us. Hundreds of lights illumined the room. There were two rows of barrels of 250 gallons each, and upon the end of each was a sperm candle lighted. The barrels being of an equal size, the effect was very fine. This first cellar is about 100 feet long, 40 feet wide, and 25 feet high. It contains several rows of barrels, of which only the two in the centre were lighted. From this we reached a still larger cellar, built square, with the arches resting upon a fine column in the centre. The barrels are placed in a circle, leaving a large space of about thirty feet vacant. Each barrel bore a lighted candle, which added still more to the grandeur of the effect. Around the central column is a table, on which were placed about forty glasses for tasting the wine. From this cellar there is still another, which also was lighted. It is about 100 feet in length.

Upon returning to the middle cellar we stopped at the table before-mentioned; the deputy then ordered wine to be brought from the year 1822 to 1859: beyond this year the wines are not presentable. The reader may imagine with what caution we put ourselves to the task of tasting. To describe the wines would be a work sufficient for Byron, Shakspeare, or Schiller, and even those geniuses would not do full justice to them until they had imbibed a couple of glasses full. As you take a mouthful and let it run drop by drop down your throat, it leaves in your mouth the same aroma as a bouquet of the choicest flowers will offer to your olfactories.

The older a wine becomes, the less grows its bouquet, but it grows more and more delicate. A young wine of four years old has this bouquet in a very great degree; but as it becomes older it loses it, gaining instead a more delicate but more penetrating taste; it now communicates to the palate slowly but surely its perfume.

After having tasted many, we finally concluded by drinking a couple of glasses of the finest wine mortal can imbibe. I may here remark to those who are not initiated in the manner of *tasting* wine, that you do not drink it, but take a few drops on your tongue, and if it is old, let a few drops trickle slowly down your throat. If the wine is of little value, you keep it a few moments in your mouth and then throw it out. The reason of this is that a fine old wine will, by a few drops, give you the entire taste, whereas it is necessary to take a large mouthful of the inferior wine in order to be able to judge of its quality. The Duke every year causes a public auction to be held; then wines of three and four years old are sold. Older wines are not sold at public auction, but have a fixed price, which would astonish some of my readers. Again, there are wines which can not be bought for any price.

The wines grown on different parts of the domain are kept in this cellar. The grapes are picked by women and children, who have wooden tubs with leathern straps, so that they may be carried on the back. When these tubs are full, they are taken to a place where there are persons who classify the grapes; that is, they take all the finest bunches and lay them on one side, then the next finest, and so on; from these latter sorts the second and third class wine is made. From the first class grapes (which are allowed to become like raisins before they are picked), the finest berries are cut out and placed in a large earthenware dish; from these selected grapes is made the first class wine called the Auslese ("Select"). These grapes are trodden out with boots made for that purpose. They are pressed in a press of their own, so that no other juice may be mixed with theirs. The juice is then put into a clean barrel and left for fermentation. The bung-hole is covered with an earthenware funnel, which is half filled with water, so that the gas bubbles up through the water, but lets no air reach the wine. This precaution is used with all wines, none being fermented with bung-holes open.

The first class bunches, from which the finest berries have already been picked, are then trodden, pressed, and produce the second quality. To this is also put that juice which is pressed from the best of the second and third class bunches; that is, from each of the bunches the finest berries are cut out, as from the first class.

Seeing in the cellar barrels containing but 170 to 250 gallons each, I asked whether they considered the wine better in a small barrel or in a large one, say of 2000 gallons.

The answer was that the wine is much better in a large barrel, as the fermentation then is more uniform. But they are troubled to fill one of the large barrels with wine of the first quality. The Steinberg vineyard of 104 *morgen* will, in a very good season (which is once in about ten years), fill with first class wine one stück, or 250 gallons. In other years it is with difficulty that they can fill a half stück.

It is now admitted by every one here that fine wine-making depends as much on the careful selection and classification of the grapes and their quality as upon the climate and soil. Even in places where very inferior wine was raised formerly, now, by careful selection of grapes, care, and attention during the fermentation, fine wine is made, which frequently sells for 1500 to 2000 *güldens* per barrel. The above has been proved by the experience of the veteran officer of the cellars, who some time ago celebrated the fiftieth year in the service of his government, exclusively in the superintendence of vineyards and vines. Having begun as cup-bearer, he rose by degrees to his present position. With regard to the fermentation, I was told that the wine will ferment from ten to twelve days. The warm or cold weather has much to do with the length of time required for the fermentation.

The grapes are generally picked at the end of November and beginning of December, often when the snow is two, and even three inches thick on the ground; but if they are caught by snow or rain, they lose much of their beauty, and the wine its flavor.

In the press-house there are about thirty presses. They consist of a simple screw, which has two rings to put in the lever end.

This lever is a long oak pole, within fifteen feet of the press. There is an upright on a pivot. This upright has holes made through, long enough to receive levers to turn the same. It acts altogether like a capstan on a vessel. The presses are simple, and susceptible of great improvement. After inspecting every thing in the cellar and press-house, we went to take a country dinner in the cooper's room. It was served up by a rosy-cheeked girl. After giving her two thalers, and the cooper who served the wine in the cellar five thalers, we left for Johannisberg, the palace of the Prince Metternich.

The palace of the prince is about two hours' drive from Eberbach. The country lying between these two celebrated vineyards gradually rises from the River Rhine. With the exception of Steinberg and its immediate vicinity, the soil is a very red clay, heavily intermixed with gravel. This is the same soil as Sonoma possesses by thousands of acres, and in other parts of California there are millions. Of course, every spot of earth is planted here; and so economical are they with the ground, that the walks are not more than three or four feet wide. The vineyard lots are small, from a quarter of an acre to two acres. I asked the director the price of one *morgen*. He answered that they have no price, as it is all owned by rich people of all countries, none of whom will sell. For many years there has been no instance of a sale. If a division takes place among heirs, and the vineyard is so small that it can not be divided, the *morgen* is valued at 20,000 *güldens*, and the retainer of the vineyard has to pay over to the other heir his part of the money.

After passing several prosperous villages, we arrived at last at the palace. The courteous steward received us very kindly. Mr. Joh. Herzmansky has been for many years the manager of this beautiful property. The palace is about three miles from the River Rhine, and is situated upon an elevation. As you step upon the terrace in front of the palace, a grand and beautiful view meets your gaze. The Prince may boast of the view from his palace, as I can from my ranch in Sonoma; or, rather, I may boast of having scenery equal to that of the Prince Metternich. It is true that I have no River Rhine, but in its place there lies the St. Pablo Bay.

The vineyard encircles the palace and contains sixty-five *morgen*. Some spots are newly planted; some lie fallow, as here also the vines will produce for thirty years only, when they are cut out, and the ground suffered to rest for three or four years, well manured, and then replanted.

Here the vines look very well, having a good healthy color, and are kept clean, no grass being visible. The grapes show signs of ripening. They are all of one kind—the Riesling. There are several varieties of table grapes in the yards and around the walks in the garden, but in the vineyard there are no varieties.

We were then invited to walk into the cellars, which are under the palace. After going down thirty feet we entered the first cellar, which was lighted in the same manner as that of the Duke previously described, with the exception that it is not round. The vaults are all about forty feet wide and twenty high, arched with stone. This domain originally belonged to the priests, and was a monastery, but Napoleon drove out the monks and presented their abode to Kellerman, one of his generals. After the deposition of Napoleon the Congress of Vienna presented Prince Metternich with this domain for his services. The deceased and the present prince have spent much in beautifying this truly royal domain.

We tasted many wines, which *must* be tasted to know their magnificence, for it is beyond the power of description. These wines, like those of the Duke of Nassau, are occasionally sold at public auction, but at such exorbitant prices that we poor republicans would shudder as much to drink such costly liquid as if it was molten gold. There is a pardonable rivalry existing between the officers of the Duke of Nassau and those of Prince Metternich. Those of the Duke contend that the Steinberg gives the best wine, whereas those of the Prince say the Johannisberg is better. This divided opinion is held all over the country among the citizens. Both vineyards have the same kind of grape, the Riesling, so it is but the location and the soil which can be in favor of the one or the other. The mode of making the wine is the same, but the grapes are not always picked at the same time; for instance, Mr. Herzmansky, in 1849, plucked his grapes a week earlier than the master of the cellars of the Duke. During that week some snow fell, which watered the Duke's grapes, and, though he made magnificent wine, still it is not considered as good as that of Johannisberg. This lucky stroke of his superintendent benefited the owner of Johannisberg many thousand *gülldens*. From the first-selected berries they made one barrel of 175 gallons, for which they refused 12,000 *gülden*. The wines are here sold after being four days or three years old.   The prices are almost the same as those at Eberbach.

Beyond the first cellar is another, built in the same shape as the first.   We did not enter it, as it is only used for fermenting the new wines, and of course it is at present empty.   The cellars extend all around the large palace.   After we had finished tasting the wines, our host made us empty a couple of glasses to the prosperity of the vine culture in California.   After doing this it was with difficulty that we could leave our courteous host, who insisted upon our drinking still more; but I summoned up virtue to decline, though I am afraid it will be many a long year before such precious nectar will again moisten my lips.   The general opinion is that wines will attain their greatest excellence in from five to ten years, and after that they lose much of their splendid and acquired bouquet.

On leaving the cellar, and presenting the cooper with sixteen thalers, we entered the carriage and drove toward home, passing Biberich, where we left Mr. Victor.   We arrived in Wiesbaden quite late in the night, after having had the honor of tasting the finest wines in Europe, for to my palate there are no finer than the above-named.

August 27.—This morning Mr. Thomä called, and stated that he had ordered the list of sales for the last three years to be made out.   And now he was ready to take me to Geisberg, where the agricultural Experimental Gardens are located.   Here there is a vineyard of about 300 kinds of grapes which are tested.   The principal care is used in testing the mode of pruning, and raising the vines low or high, setting them in rows or squares, staking them, or training them over wires in trellis form, and the like. Many experiments are made upon the vines.   Each row is kept apart, raised, pruned, trimmed separately.   The progress of the vine and grape is closely watched by experienced chemists; the leaves, wood, and grape are chemically analyzed to see what difference is made by the different modes of cultivation.   The grapes are gathered on the same day, divided into three classes from each row; then they are equally tested, from time to time, with the alcometer.   In this way, from year to year, this systematic experimenting goes on.   I was told that, so far, the low trimming, or, in other words, vines raised just high enough to prevent the grapes from hanging on the ground, is the best mode of raising them.   This proves the truth of my experience with regard to

California vines, with the exception that we need not fear to have our grapes upon the ground, as there are no summer rains with us. In the garden hops, grains, and vegetables are planted. The Agricultural School is supported by the State. It possesses models of all utensils invented here, a fine agricultural library, and collections of grains, seeds, and objects of Natural History.

I presented the Director with two volumes of our State agricultural reports. I found here a copy of the Patent Office reports of 1846. I promised to send some later numbers, and I also made arrangements to exchange seeds, etc., with the Institute. After examining every thing, and taking down the names of various books on wine culture, I returned to my hotel, where I wrote a letter of thanks to Director Thomä and the chief master of the cellars. I thanked them in the name of our government; for it was to California I owed the distinguished reception I met as her commissioner. I then packed up my things, and, after parting with my new acquaintances, and especially from Director Thomä —to whom I would here again express my sincere thanks for his courtesy, and the information he so freely and kindly furnished— I took the cars for Frankfort, having previously dispatched my son to Ems to escort his mother and sister to Mayence, where I expected to meet them.

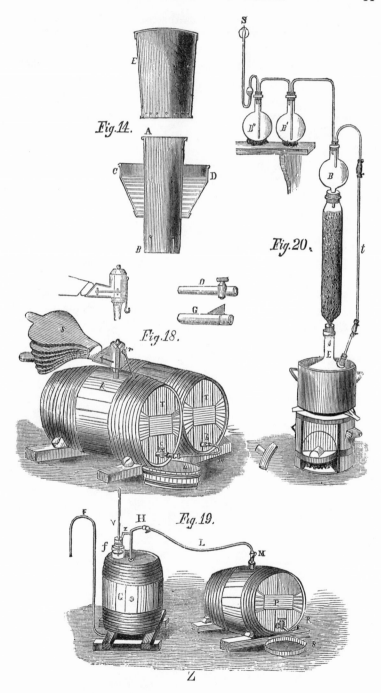

Fig.14.

Fig.18.

Fig.20.

Fig.19.

CHAPTER V.

GERMANY, THROUGH SWITZERLAND, TO ITALY.

From Frankfort to Mayence.—The Russian Lady and her Maid.—Her extra Baggage.—Our Talk about California.—European Ideas of our State.—Hints for the Press of California.—Wash dirty Linen at Home.—Chronicle on Normal Progress rather than on exceptional Crimes.—Mayence to Heidelberg.—Tobacco.—Heidelberg.—Nursery at Wiesloch.—Carl Brunner.—His Nursery, Gardens, and Vineyard.—His Wine-press.—The great Tun at Heidelberg.—Start for Basle.—Notes by the Way.—Hemp.—Manuring by Burning.—From Basle to Geneva.—Neufchatel.—The Swiss and American Lakes.—Geneva.—Passports for Italy.—Americans in Geneva.—Departure for Italy.—The Road and the Country.—St. Jean de Moreno.—The Tunnel.—Crossing the Summit.—The Descent.—Arrival at Turin.

August 27.—On entering the cars at Frankfort for Mayence, I was much amused with a lady from Russia, in the same car with me, returning from the baths at Wiesbaden. Her servant-girl, not speaking a word of German, soon got into trouble about the innumerable boxes, packages, bundles, umbrellas, parasols, and many other things placed in her charge, all of which were to be taken into the cars, as this formidable pile contained but a few little extras to be kept near at hand. The main and heavy baggage, to the amount of fourteen tickets, which I saw, was already in the baggage-car. The bundles had to go into the car, and after the seat and the net-work on the top were filled, in came the mistress herself, laden with a goodly number more, which she piled up above her and in her lap. The conductor rushed forward, telling the maid to go in. She gesticulated, and talked to him in Russian, he not understanding a word of her language. She was at last put in the place she was to occupy, the conductor taking her by the arm and shoving her into the car. This started the lady herself, who at best knew but few German words. A rush was made by both mistress and maid for the luggage which still lay at the door of the car. The first whistle sounded. The conductor endeavored to close the car door, seeing that the ladies were almost crazy. Having had enough amusement already, I took pity on the strangers, and told the conductor that these *few* traps belonged to them, and that they wished to take them in the car. He looked very much puzzled, and asked me whether they belonged to an opera troupe traveling to some interior town. Time was scarce. He looked into the car, calculating how many seats the luggage would occupy. Finding that, even if one half the car was vacated, there would be scarcely room enough, he put the two ladies into the car, and, with the help of two of his companions, who came to see what was the matter, gathered up the packages and bundles, and threw them into the post-wagon. The whistle sounded, and away we went.

I knew from my travels in old times that Russian ladies were fast talkers, but I never had the least idea of the rapidity exhibited by these two; and I believe that as Russia is improving rapidly in all its movements, these two ladies endeavored to imitate the speed of the telegraph. The mistress accused the maid of slowness in not taking in the bundles quick enough, saying, "Now all is lost, and never will be recovered again." The maid defended herself, saying how impossible it would have been to have taken them all in, adding, "I told you so, madam. How lucky it was that young master sent the greater portion of the baggage as freight, by steamer, up the Rhine!" This remark by the maid raised a smile on my countenance which I could not suppress. I told the lady not to be worried, that the baggage was all safe, that the conductor had put them in the post-car, and when they stopped all would be delivered to them. This information seemed to relieve them.

I wanted to ask her how many years she had spent in this part of Germany. This question the reader would justify if he had seen the number of boxes and packages, the fourteen tickets for trunks, and had heard the remark of the maid that her young master had sent the bulk of the baggage as freight. The lady kindly informed me that she came for her health to the several watering-places, and had been here for two months, and was now returning home. I congratulated her on her speedy recovery of health, as she looked a picture of good health. But she differed very much with me in that respect, stating that she was very delicate, and continued so much so that she even refused to go with her brother to Paris, though she *did* need dresses very much. She was a *widow*.

Thanking me for my aid in making the conductor understand their embarrassment, she asked me what part of Germany I was from. My answer that I was a Californian seemed to astonish her. Every body in the car looked at me, and I became the lion of the time. My fair neighbor asked me many questions about the gold; how long I had lived in California, and so on. I told her eleven years. "Why," she said, "and you have not been killed! How have you escaped so many years without having been murdered? But," she added, "may be you had a strong guard around you." I told her that, living in the country, far from any neighbors, my doors were never locked night or day. She heard all this with great surprise, asking how it was that newspapers gave so many accounts of murders in America, particularly in California. The gentlemen passengers sitting in the cars, with inquiring looks, evidently desiring to hear my reply to this question, I explained to her that whenever a murder is committed the local paper will chronicle it, and neighboring papers in the towns and cities repeat it, so that it appears to the foreigner that each announcement refers to a different murder. I remarked, too, that we had no more murders than other nations, but that with us every murder, suicide, or railroad accident is published far and wide, whereas in European countries no such thing is done. I asked her whether in St. Petersburg, Moscow, etc., the dead houses are ever empty? whether it is not often the case that ten or fifteen persons are lying in these places, stretched out by the hand of murder or suicide? whether this is not the case even in the best governed, politest city in the world—Paris, never a day passing that dozens are not found in the Seine? But who hears of these casualties? Nobody save he who is in search of one lost, or some stranger who goes to see them, led by curiosity. This seemed to satisfy the lady as well as the rest of the company.

But now to the gentlemen of the press of this State a few lines, which I hope they will take kindly. It is concerning the practice of copying accounts of murders, suicides, and robberies from other papers; of re-echoing, multiplying, and, in fact, spreading the facts as far and wide as possible, so doing great injury and injustice to our young State. Some of our papers are not satisfied with such occurrences in our own State, but they will take these accounts from the papers of Oregon, Washington Territory, and Washoe. These places are not known in Europe, but California is well known; consequently, these publications are at the expense of our State alone. This is even the case in the Eastern States. For instance, a San Francisco paper states: "We extract from the *Portland Courier*" (or whatever the name may be) such and such an account of a murder. The reader in Europe or in the Eastern States does not know where Portland is; he has read it in a San Francisco paper, and therefore thinks it in California. But the zeal and energy of newspaper men does not end here. Some will carefully register all crimes committed, and publish them quarterly, half yearly, or annually. Others go still farther. The divorce cases, lawsuits, names of bankrupts, are summed up and published half yearly or yearly. If this collection of our vices, so carefully collected, which we send broadcast to the world, is intended to scare off emigration, no better method could be in-. vented. It is certain that the press does not desire this, but publishes without considering what effect it may have on the other side of the world. I suppose the intention is to chastise, mortify, and expose these crimes to our own people. This would be very well if other countries did the same to their own people; but, as Napoleon said, when a row was kicked up about an illegitimate child in the family of a noble and the case was brought before him, "The husband of the wife must be the father of the wife's children before the world. Dirty linen must be washed in the family." If, then, other nations wash their dirty linen in secret, and we do it openly, other nations will have considerable advantage over us in the eyes of the world. This was by no means the only time while traveling in Europe that I heard mentioned the immense number of crimes which occur in California. In fact, it is only known for its gold and its crimes.

Why do not the papers chronicle with the same minuteness accounts of our material and commercial progress. Give the statistics of our agriculture and manufactures. They would then astonish the civilized world with the unparalleled wealth, prosperity, industry, and energy of our really wonderful people. If the press will bestow the same labor in statistical reports as they do in reporting crimes, I warrant that, in a short time, California and its great and various wealth will be truly known all over Europe; and as no country on the face of the globe can really offer the same advantages in so many and various ways to men of industry and of wealth, soon a population will flow in, from all parts, of all professions and occupations, filling our cities, tilling our valleys, mountains, and plains. Who has read "Robinson Crusoe," and has not desired to travel and see the world? Where is the man who has read descriptions of London, Paris, or Rome, and does not desire to visit them? But how can a man desire to emigrate to a country from which he has heard nothing but tales of crime, of which he knows only the bad side? But I will leave this topic and return to my journey.

August 28.—At one o'clock we left Mayence for Heidelberg. Immediately upon leaving Mayence we saw some vineyards upon very steep hills. The ground was walled up. After proceeding along for some miles, we entered a large, wide plain. It is very well cultivated, and divided into very small lots, well planted with fruit-trees. The grain is all harvested, but the stubble shows barley, oats, and wheat. There are yet potatoes, hemp, and occasionally a patch of tobacco. The closer we approached Manheim the thicker grew the tobacco-plots. After leaving the ancient city of Manheim, the ground was principally planted with tobacco, which is small, not being higher than about eighteen inches to two feet. I saw but two qualities, the long-leaved or Hungarian tobacco, and the round-leaved, or what we call the Kentucky seedling. Judging from the size of the plant, I hardly think that more than 600 pounds can be raised here to the acre.

At four o'clock P.M. we arrived at Heidelberg. I hear there is a nursery in the vicinity; and as it is the first one I have found since I left America, I will reserve this treat for my birthday.

August 29.—This day was spent in arranging my correspondence and bringing up my journal. This evening we took a walk to see the celebrated Heidelberg ruins, which are still in a tolerable state of preservation; but, as it was no part of my mission to examine and describe old ruins, I pass them by.

August 30.—Having traveled almost all over Germany, and considerably out of my way, to find a nursery, I am at last to be gratified. At three o'clock we started for Wiesloch. Upon arriving there, we immediately went to Mr. Carl Brunner, the person recommended to us by Director Thomä. We found him at home. Upon telling him my errand, he immediately took me to his nurseries and vineyards, located at some distance from town. The nurseries are in small strips; for here, as almost all over Germany, every man has his land in several places and in small strips. For instance, Mr. Brunner has over sixty *morgens*, and in about eighty different pieces. This is very troublesome business, and has but one advantage—that when a hail-storm comes, as it is only in streaks, it does not take the whole of any one man's land. We examined many of his nurseries and a part of his vineyards. His catalogue contains over 400 varieties of

F

grape-vines, but I selected only such as are raised in this neighborhood, amounting to 100 varieties, according to the catalogue.
The vineyards showed but a poor crop, or, in fact, no crop at all;
as the frost so killed the vines in the spring that a *morgen* with
4600 vines will not give fifty gallons of wine. But still these
people do well; for when there is a good year, it pays them well
for all their trouble and expense during the bad ones.

After visiting the vineyards, we went to see the venerable Mr.
Brunner, who has written a valuable book upon the grape and
the making of red wine. For fifty years he has been engaged in
collecting the most celebrated varieties of vines from all countries, but in later years he has given his nursery and collection
up to his son and retired, only retaining the business of buying
and selling wine.

The old gentleman is a learned man, and well merits the esteem
he possesses of the larger part of Germany. He is a great ama-
teur of roses and flowers in general, and he has a garden of considerable size, where he has collected over one thousand varieties
of roses. In this favorite place of his we found the old man. He
is lively, pleasant, cheerful, and content. He showed us his garden, and opposite it a vineyard which is thirty years old, and has
several varieties of vines planted, but each in a separate lot.
Here, as elsewhere, the frost has destroyed this year's crop. The
vines are raised on a trellis, not tied to stakes; but small sticks
are driven down about five or six feet apart; then other sticks,
mostly split from poplar, are tied to the upright stakes. This
makes a kind of trellis. In some parts, where wood is more distant, and consequently costlier, the cross-pieces, instead of being
wood, are wire; and it is to this that the grape-vines are tied.
This trellis-work is about three to three and a half feet high. The
opinion in respect to this mode is divided. Those districts which
raise their vines on sticks contend that their method is the best.
Those that have trellises are in favor of their own mode. One
thing is clear to me—that the vines raised on straight sticks are
easiest to work; for when you are in a row of trellised vines, you
are obliged to go to the end before you can enter another row;
besides, the shade on the trellis must be more than on the other.

August 31.—The vineyard of the old gentleman is on a side
hill, quite steep, but not so much so as to prevent a person climbing it without steps. The soil is red, containing much gravel—
is volcanic. Clay is its general characteristic. There is a great

deal of red wine made here, but more white. The wines have a good reputation, but are not classed as "Number One."

The fermentation of the white wine is the same as already described. The vineyards being small, and belonging to poor people, the selecting of grapes is very little practiced; and this is the reason why no such fine wine is here made as in Hochheim, Steinberg, Johannisberg, etc. Still, even here the people pick out the rotten grapes, leaves, and unripened bunches, as they would greatly injure the wine.

Mr. Brunner also showed me his wine-press, upon which he prides himself, it being more compact and occupying less space than the usual presses. It is furnished with one large iron screw, which is turned at the top with two levers which reach to the outside of the press-box, so that the operator may walk around the box pushing or pulling the levers. The advantage lies not so much in the screw as in the mode of filling the press, which is done in the following manner: The box is filled about one foot, when the screw is turned hard down on the mass. When this is well pressed the screw is raised, and another foot is placed upon the first mass and also pressed. The wood pieces upon which the screw presses are then taken up, but the plank with holes bored through, which forms the top piece on the mass, is left, and on this is placed a tier of stems, seeds, and grapes, to a thickness of a foot; and upon this, again, a wood piece is placed on which the screw presses, and the operation is carried on as before. Thus every particle of juice is pressed out of the lower mass, which is then taken out, and the upper mass takes its place.

After examining every thing sufficiently, we started again for Heidelberg, where we arrived at 11 o'clock A.M. The whole day was occupied in continuing my correspondence. In the evening I went to see the great tun of Heidelberg—the largest in the world. I extract the description of it from the guide-book:

"This tun was built by the cooper John Jacob Engler the younger, in the year 1751. It is said to have cost the enormous sum of 80,000 florins, and was often filled with costly wine of the Palatinate. It is 32 feet long, 22 feet in diameter at the ends, and 23 in the centre. Its 127 staves are $9\frac{3}{4}$ inches thick, and its circular bung-hole from 3 to 4 inches in diameter; 18 wooden hoops, 8 inches thick and 15 inches broad—the different rafters of which are bound together with iron hoops and screws, but the hoops at the two extremities are 18 inches in breadth. Of the hoops that now remain there are only eight, and it is not known at the present day how the rest have disappeared. From the front as well as the back ends of the tun, bent in toward the interior to meet the pressure of the liquid, it is each time held in toward the centre in its concave form by four strong rafters, the ends of which are fastened to the bottom and to the staves by iron hoops and screws. The tun reposes upon 8 very strong wooden supporters, beautifully carved, and raised several feet from the ground. The height of the whole work is, from the floor of the cellar to its highest point, 26 feet 5 inches; and on the top, in front, there is a shield surmounted with the electoral cap on an azure field, and the initials in gold of Charles Theodore. This mighty tun surpasses in size all its predecessors, for it can contain 236 fuders, or 283,000 large bottles of fluid in its colossal space. It has been three times filled with wine—in 1753, 1760, 1766. There are still to be seen in the cellar the compasses, plane, gouge, and timber mark which were used for its construction. The compasses are 8 feet 6 inches long—some verses are carved upon them; the plane is 7 feet long, 10¾ inches broad, and 4½ inches thick, with the name of the head workman carved upon it. On the top of this tun is constructed a flooring, 27 feet 7 inches above the floor of the cellar, where a numerous company may assemble to enjoy the pleasures of the dance. The vat is filled by a vertical opening in the top of the vault. There is a small iron pump over the cellar by which the tun may be emptied. In the cooperage there is another tun which holds 47 fuders. In its time of splendor this cellar is said to have contained 12 such barrels."

September 1.—We started from Heidelberg at ten o'clock for Basle. The road follows the foot of the mountains and the banks of the Rhine, which here flows into an extensive plain, which extends far beyond the reach of the eye. To the left of the railroad are high mountains rising up gradually. On their sides, about one third up, vineyards are planted all the way, which are healthy in color, and bear a good crop for this country. The mountain tops are covered with forests. Here the Schwarzwald begins. We passed many thriving villages. The plain is generally cultivated with tobacco, hemp, Indian corn, millet, hops, potatoes, and beans; but the largest portion is meadow, which is irrigated from time to time by flood-gates, which let in or keep off the water. Poplar-trees are planted around each lot in the meadow. Fields which are more elevated are planted with plums, prunes, apples, and walnuts. The latter predominates, and may be set down as one third of all the trees here planted.

The hemp, in all parts where it is planted, when ripe, is pulled out by the roots, spread upon level ground, and kept there for a couple of months. Then it is crushed with a simple wooden machine, and thus divested of the woody substance, leaving only the hemp. Some good wine is raised here; but as no particular care is taken in its manufacture, it has attained no celebrity.

Upon approaching Basle I noticed the old-fashioned way of manuring the ground by burning it. The mode is simple, and not costly where wood is cheap. The land is first plowed deeply in furrows about twenty feet apart; a small pile of wood is made of limbs, roots, etc., which is then covered with dust, and lighted like charcoal, and is kept burning slowly, now and then air-holes being made to prevent the fires going out. The people here are so expert that they do not lose the wood, but make it into charcoal; so they not only manure their land well, but also have the additional gain of a quantity of charcoal. At six o'clock P.M. we arrived in Basle—a picturesque old town, situated upon the banks of the Rhine.

September 2.—At nine o'clock we started with the cars for Geneva. The railroad runs in a narrow valley about one mile wide. The hill-sides are cultivated as grain farms, and there is only now and then a vineyard. In the valleys are meadows, irrigated by flood-gates as above described. The farm-houses are large, and built of stone; many of them are situated almost at the top of the mountain. Prunes, apples, walnuts, wheat, barley, oats, and rye are raised; also potatoes, beans, hemp, and some Indian corn. The mountain sides are well cultivated, and often large stone houses can be seen on the summit of the mountains. At Beel we changed cars, and seemingly country too, for from here the vine seemed to be the exclusive cultivation. Every foot of ground, even three fourths up the mountains, is planted with vines, which are looking well, and have a good crop. The soil is yellow clay, much intermixed with rocks and gravel. In many places rock walls are built up to hold the soil. Where the vines are growing, much labor is bestowed upon redeeming land enough to hold fifty to one hundred vines, planted three and a half feet apart, and the rows two and a half feet. In California such a piece of ground would hold only seven or nine vines (as we plant them), and would cost about $400 to make it.

We soon came to the end of the lake, where lies Neufchatel. This lake, with its mirror-like smoothness, its limpid waters, and surrounding scenery, can not fail to draw the admiration of the traveler. Still, however grand its beauty may be, it can not equal the wild grandeur of the lakes of Wisconsin or Minnesota before the hand of civilization robbed them of half their beauty. Those thousand lakes, lying calm, peaceful, under a cloudless sky; that solemn stillness; the deep dark foliage of a thousand different tints and shades in autumn—all this, when once seen, can never be forgotten, and the lakes of Switzerland lose half their beauty by the comparison.

At the village of Neufchatel we changed cars for Geneva. Near this place the soil is reddish, and its wine has some renown. The cultivation of the vine is carried on with great industry, but the soil is poor, and requires a great deal of manure. The vineyards lie three fourths up of the side of the mountains; beyond them are the fruit-trees, and near the top are either bare rocks or dense forests. We arrived in Geneva after traveling eight hours continually among vineyards from one mile to three and a half wide. Not a spot as large as an ordinary brick-yard was left uncultivated, with the exception of where the old vines have been cut out to give the ground the necessary three years' rest.

Upon our arrival at this ancient town, celebrated for its watches, we were obliged to drive around some time before we could obtain lodgings, as at present there is a convention here of ministers of all Protestant denominations. At last, however, we found rooms and a good supper, to which we did ample justice.

September 3.—Having taken a carriage, we drove around the city and along the shore of the lake which lies at its side, on the mirror-like surface of which floated dozens of swans. The bridge across the river at the lower end of the lake is a great work of art. The neighborhood of the city is picturesque; the bold, towering rocks, always capped with everlasting snow, inspire the traveler on a September day to wish himself in one of those crevices, where he might breathe an atmosphere rather lower in temperature than 85°. After seeing all the sights, we drove to the hotel, discharged the driver, and started to have our revolvers cleaned up and reloaded, as we had to cross the Alps. From thence we went to the United States Consul to have our passports viséd; not that it was required, but to avoid the annoyance of running to the Consulate, perhaps not finding the Consul in, and, above all, paying your tribute of one dollar for his signature.

Coming from the Consul we met Mr. Samuel Brannan and his lady. Mrs. Brannan, with her children, live here, in a very fine villa, surrounded by extensive grounds, adjoining the town; a more desirable residence could hardly be wished. Mr. and Mrs. Brannan kindly invited me to remain some time at their villa; but this offer I was obliged to decline, as my duty called me to work in other parts. Mr. Brannan visited me at the hotel, and we together went to visit Mrs. Hitchcock. On arriving at her residence we found that Mrs. H. was absent, but were received by Miss Hitchcock. With this young lady's graceful reception and accomplished manners we were very much struck. But time prevented us from enjoying long the pleasure of her company, as we were obliged to make haste to take the cars, which conveyed us to St. Jean de Moreno.

The road runs a long time on the banks of the River Rhone, and at the foot of a range of hills, which are planted thickly with vines. I noticed that some of them were planted four feet apart, and without sticks, as mine are in Sonoma. The vines were not pruned, and were well filled with grapes for this country. Occasionally I saw some staked vineyards, as if opinions differed as to the best mode; but the unstaked were the most prevalent.

On reaching the French line we were stopped, and got out to have our trunks and passports examined; but as I passed the official without even giving him a look, he allowed me to go on without a question. The trunks of my party were merely brought in and taken out without the slightest investigation. This being the limit of the Sardinian territory lately annexed by Napoleon to France, we soon saw something of the Italian mode of cultivating the vine, which is planted by a small tree, and allowed to run entirely over it, making it resemble a diminutive haystack. The rows are about 100 to 120 feet apart. In this space is planted grain or Indian corn, of which much is here raised. On the lake side vines are extensively raised in the manner before described. Mulberry-trees also begin to make their appearance, sometimes with grapes running over them, and sometimes furnishing food for the silk-worm.

Night soon set in, and nothing could be seen but a few lights dancing about on the towering mountains at whose base we passed. At half past eight o'clock we arrived at St. Jean, which is the terminus of the present railroad. The hotel at which we stopped was only a few minutes' walk from the station, but the town itself is a quarter of an hour's walk.

September 4.—Early this morning I went to hire a carriage to take us across the Alps. I succeeded, and we started at seven o'clock, keeping along the banks of the rapid stream. The scenery is thoroughly grand: high mountains covered with the stately pine; huge rocks towering above us, as if on the eve of falling to crush the intruders; thousands of waterfalls, which resembled from a distance a silver ribbon; in the far-off distance, mountains clad with perpetual snow. There are many coal-mines on the road, and villages which seem above the clouds. The land from one rod up to five rods is all worked, but without oxen, mule, or horse, as the inhabitants work their small property with spades. Only a few vines may be seen now and then.

September 5.—The tunnel which is now being constructed will, when finished, connect Italy and France, and will be four and a half leagues in length. They are now pumping air into it, as the workmen suffer much from its want. We passed within half a mile of it, but as it was not connected with my commission I did not visit it. After riding four miles more we stopped at a small village and took our dinner. The mountains begin to show more and more snow; still, right under these snow-banks may be seen houses, and herds of cattle grazing. Terrace upon terrace is built from five to eighteen feet, according to the steepness of the hills. This flat of ground is gained by walling up the side of the mountain, and then carefully filling the space with sifted ground gravel, and the manure which the poor peasant treasures up with great care during the whole year. The crops raised on these patches of land are brought down on the backs of men and women.

On this road is the Fort St. Albert; the old one was blown up by Napoleon. The mountains began to become more and more distinct with their masses of snow. The cascades were more and more numerous. At last we arrived in the village, where we were to remain all night. Next morning, on the arrival of the stage, I found that the poor travelers were almost frozen with cold, which was intense during the night in the valleys and deep ravines of the snow-clad mountains.

At seven o'clock we started. Four mules were placed to the carriage, as here the road begins to rise from the plain to the mountain. The road winds so gradually around the mountain, and is in such excellent order, that one hardly feels the gradual rise. It was constructed by Napoleon, and the French side is kept by that government; the Italian by Victor Emanuel. At a distance of every half mile there are men who water the road from morning till night from a small ditch which runs alongside, and which is supplied with water by the thousands of natural falls. The man on the road is furnished with a huge wooden shovel resembling a ladle; with this he throws the water over the entire way.

When about one fourth up the mountain I got out of the carriage, and walked across the summit of the Alps, arriving on the opposite side at a tavern about ten minutes sooner than the carriage. Near this tavern is a small lake, on the border of which Napoleon had some breast-works built. There is also the old hospital which he erected for his wounded soldiers.

We soon continued our journey at a slow trot, never fatiguing the horses. The reader may judge how gradual is the descent when I say the small ditch at the side of the road runs steadily at a rate of four miles an hour. At two o'clock we arrived at Susa. At the gate a custom-house officer mounted on the carriage, and took us to the railroad station, where is also the custom-house. The officers politely passed our trunks without opening them, and informed us that we could leave them there with perfect security. Therefore we went to a hotel, took an excellent dinner, and, at five o'clock, started for Turin, where we arrived at seven.

After taking rooms we went out for a stroll, passing the King's palace, where there were several carriages in waiting. The salons were all finely lighted up, and, as the windows were open, we were enabled to see some large oil paintings. However, as we were very tired, we soon returned to our rooms, and sought our beds.

CHAPTER VI.

ITALY :—WINE AND SILK.

Turin.—Passports.—Leave for Genoa.—Vines and Mulberries.—Plowing.—Grain Crops.—Manuring.—Asti and its Wines.—Reach Genoa.—The Birthplace of Columbus.—Narrow Streets.—Professor Isnard.—Procure Vines.—Nova.—The Silk Manufactory.—Jealousy of Visitors.—Scanty Information.—Raising Silkworms.—Return.—Effects of Asti Wine.—Return to Genoa.—Wine-making in Italy.—No Berths for Civita Vecchia.—Leave for Marseilles.—The Voyage.—Laying by.—Extra Charge for Board.—Arrival at Marseilles.

September 6.—Finding that nothing in the way of wine or silk raising can be done in Turin, I started this day for Genoa, through the town of Asti, where the best wine of modern Italy is said to be made. Before leaving Turin I thought it would be better to have my passport viséd by the Pope's embassador, therefore I sent it to that officer, but was surprised to hear that I must first go to the American minister, as he had officially requested him and all other ministers not to visé any American passports unless first seen and viséd by himself. I then sent the servant to the American minister, who requested me to call upon him. This annoyed me considerably; but still, as it had to be done, and as I intended to call upon the minister anyhow, I went, and was received kindly. He apologized for putting me to so much trouble, but such were his instructions with regard to all. He signed our passports without charge; and, thanking him, we bowed ourselves out, and went to the Pope's embassador, who made no farther trouble.

Turin is the present residence of Victor Emanuel. It is a handsome city, the houses being built in modern style, the streets wide and clean. Some fine public squares adorn the city, also some fine fountains; but, above all, it is very conveniently built for a hot climate. Its side-walks are almost all arched over, so that one may go almost all over the city without being exposed to the sun or rain.

At three o'clock we left Turin. Here the country is rolling hills, more yellow clay than sand. On these hills are planted grape-vines; in the valley, fields; and the fields are surrounded by mulberry-trees, of which, each year, the growth of the last is trimmed off, so that there shall be new and more tender leaves for the food of the silk-worm. As the tree is low, the leaves do not spread, and are easily gathered. The production of silk here is very extensive and profitable. When I reach Genoa I shall examine this subject thoroughly.

The vines on the hills are planted in two different ways—some by trees, and allowed to run over them; the others by trellis-work. Both seem to do well; the vines hang full of grapes.

The plowing in the plains is done with the limb of a tree shod with iron, and drawn by a yoke of oxen. It is wonderful how with this ancient Roman plow they can strike such beautiful furrows. They are now summer-fallowing for putting in wheat, and they do it beautifully. But it is very difficult, and but little can be plowed in the day.

The wheat, which they thresh with flails, is all the bearded red kind, known in California as the "Mediterranean wheat." It is a sure crop, and never mildews or rots. Much Indian corn is raised here; it is the deep-yellow corn, almost red. Millet for consumption is also raised in large quantities. Now and then a small patch of sugar-cane can be seen, but I suppose that is more for fancy than profit. Will my readers believe that these people are so far back in improvements that they have no fanning-mill, but, as in olden times, clean their grain by throwing it against the wind, and then sweeping it together, so that the husks not taken off by the wind are swept off by the broom?

I also observed that they plant poplar-trees in the meadow around the small lots, so that the falling leaves shall manure the ground. I likewise noticed that burned earth was brought from some other part of the property, and laid upon the ground for amelioration. It is said to increase the crop by one half.

The town of Asti, from which the wine of that name comes, is situated in a rolling country, the hills being small, none being higher than Telegraph Hill of San Francisco. The soil is yellow clay, with no gravel. It is about one third sand. The wine here raised is by no means considered generous, but it is cheap and pleasant, as it has not the bitter taste of the French or Hungarian wines. It is light, and excellent to drink in a hot climate. I emptied a bottle with good will, and almost at one draught. The wine had no intoxicating effect upon me. It is principally red wine. The white is not so good, being more sweet and stronger. Champagne is also made from these grapes.

Leaving Asti, the land continues to be undulating, and the vine-yards are the same until Solero. Gelezzano has the same wine as Asti in the plains, but mulberry-trees and grain are the chief produce; still, the vines never fail, and abundantly remunerate the planter. Not the slightest attention is paid to the selection of grapes or their fermentation. I understand, however, that there is a gentleman who has attended to wine-making, and that he was successful in making a generous wine. I will return to Asti, dis-cover his whereabouts, and get as much information as possible, for the Asti vines will improve on our red soil.

After leaving Solero we entered a large plain, extending as far as the eye can reach. This plain is all planted with mulber-ry-trees. We passed the strong Fort Alexandria and several small villages; but darkness soon set in, and I could see nothing of the country. We also passed through several tunnels, some of them four or five miles long, judging from the time it took us to pass through.

At half past nine in the evening we arrived in Genoa, and were taken to the ancient building now occupied by the Hotel Feder. The apartments are truly fine, from thirty to thirty-five feet square, and finely arched, the ceiling being twenty feet high in the centre. It is also frescoed, and the walls are painted in the same. The cornices are finely gilded, and the rooms contain massive ancient furniture.

September 7.—After writing my journal I began to make in-quiries as to where I could see silk manufactories and where con-tract for vines. The accommodating host promised to furnish me to-morrow with all the necessary introductions, so there was noth-ing left to do but to roam through this old city, the birthplace of Columbus.

It has a fine inclosed harbor, where lie hundreds of small craft trading on the coast. The wharves are scenes of busy confusion. Men half naked are here employed from morning till night in loading and unloading vessels, and drawing heavy weights on a car on low wheels. They do immense labor; still, their earnings are very small.

From the quay I turned my steps to the interior of the city, which I found beyond description—the streets about six to eight feet wide, very irregular; the houses on each side five and six

stories high, dark and dirty-looking, and from the windows of
the houses the neighbors may reach over and shake hands. A
person may imagine that such a street has not the sweetest odor
in the world. No wagons can go in the streets, nor are there
many used, as men do the work of horses and mules. Still, there
are a few of the latter seen sometimes. When they are loaded
with a bulky substance, a person meeting one finds himself in a
very precarious situation in the narrow streets; and if there is
not a doorway or a cross-street near by, it is a question whether
he or the donkey will remain master of the field. The shops in
these streets are dark, and the mechanics work almost continually
by the light of a lamp. There are a few openings in this city,
which can not be called squares, but only spaces of 100 feet, in
the most irregular form possible. I found several *no-shaped*
places, where they sell vegetables and fruit. These were fresh,
and excellent. The almonds, oranges, and lemons look very fine;
the white fig is delicious.

September 8.—I took a carriage and started out with Professor
R. I. Isnard to a neighboring village, and, after examining the
vines and fruit-trees in the nursery, I engaged a person at Rivara
to pack and send to me at Marseilles the following varieties of
vines: *Boseo, Melea, Bianchetto, Vermentino, Bois, Nebiolo, Bianco
de Asti, Malvoisea.* The above vines are all native to this section
of Italy. The grapes are excellent. I engaged cuttings as well
as rooted vines. After this we started for home, which we reached after a very dusty ride. When it came to paying the hack-
man, he asked double the price of what I had agreed to pay; but
as I had no time to argue, I gave what he asked and left him. I
made an arrangement with Professor Isnard to start to-morrow
morning at five o'clock to the small town of Nova to see some
silk manufactories.

September 9.—We reached Nova at eight o'clock, when we took
breakfast, and immediately started for one of the principal silk
manufactories. After much difficulty we were at last admitted,
as the overseer thought me French, of whom they are very jealous, for fear they will learn something of their silk manufactory.
With great mystery and suspicion they showed me the cocoons,
which they had in a lofty magazine. They were spread upon
cane mats, placed one above the other, upon racks made for that
purpose. From this place I could look down to where the wom-
en, about 120 in number, were at work unwinding the cocoons.

These are placed in warm water, and the end of the thread being found, it is wound upon a wheel driven by a steam-engine. Each woman has a wheel and an iron box before her; in the latter are placed the cocoons.

The overseer took great care that I should not see much from my stand; he urged me into the next room. I soon bid him good-by, telling him that I did not care much to see his machinery, as I had used the same thirty years ago, with the exception of the steam-engine; and in regard to that I told him that at any time America can send him machinery so complete that he would not need the women. The man looked astonished; but, as I was offended by his making so much mystery about nothing, I left him. We went to another man; but here also we met with the same difficulty. He was willing to show us all the cocoons, but nothing else. To my inquiries as to how many hands are required for 100 trees from six to ten years old, or how much silk is made from 100 pounds of leaves, the man gave me such unsatisfactory answers as showed that he either wished to mislead me, or he did not know any thing about it; consequently, I started off in search of some plain farmer who would give me the desired information.

At last we found a place where there were three hundred trees, which were thirty years old, according to the statement of an old lady, her son, and daughter, who all answered me at once. Imagine me in an Italian peasant's house, surrounded by the four inhabitants and many others, who were wondering what the strangers wanted; why they examined the mulberry-trees so closely, and so forth; and you will understand that it required a little patience to wait for the answers of these people. I asked the old lady how many pounds of cocoons she makes from the trees; at what price she sells the same; how many ounces of eggs and seeds she uses; how much labor, etc. The whole family at once kindly answered all questions but the two last, which seemed to strike them with astonishment. The idea that they should know how much labor is necessary, or how many leaves are used to an ounce of eggs, seemed something preposterous.

I was obliged to have recourse to the most roundabout ways in the world to ascertain that in some years they get 1000 francs, in others 2000, and sometimes as many as 4000 francs from the 300 trees. The labor takes about four to five weeks, when it is all finished. The family do it all themselves, and even the four are not kept busy the whole day. When the leaves begin to grow in spring, and when they have attained their full size, they put a certain quantity of eggs under the mattress upon which they sleep: the bodily heat hatches the eggs. Then some leaves are cut up very fine and put in a dish. Several whole leaves are then put above the young worms, who creep upon them. They are then laid in the dish, and begin to eat. As they grow, the leaves are cut up less fine, and the worms are placed in larger dishes, until they are placed on cane mats suspended from the ceiling. They must be regularly fed, and a great deal.

Rain-storms, or much lightning, will sometimes kill a whole brood. When the worms are ready to wind themselves, some dry weeds are stuck in the mats; the mature worm ascends and spins himself in. This is all the information I gathered from these people, who kindly and willingly told me all they could. Still, I should never have been able to understand them if I had not known the whole operation before; for I raised silk-worms on a large scale, and in the most approved manner, on my domain in Hungary. But I was willing to give my readers the manner in which these people raise the worm. I will give a more detailed description, as I intend to investigate the matter fully in the silk-growing districts in the south of France. After presenting the lady with a five-franc piece, I took my leave of her, but not before showing her a piece of quartz, and telling her that gold was found in such stones in California. Her astonishment it would be impossible to describe.

I hurried to the dépôt in order to be in time for the steamer in Genoa, which was to arrive from Marseilles, and go to Civita Vecckia. I would here stop with my journal, and only continue it from Genoa, but I must make a statement, which, though personal, gave me a piece of information concerning the wines made here.

As I before stated, upon our arrival at Nova we had taken breakfast and a bottle of wine, which was Asti white wine. We between us emptied about half the bottle, as it was very sweet, sparkling like Champagne. It had a fine bouquet, but was made without care or system.

Soon after starting with the train I felt a terrible pain coming upon me. I suffered intensely. I could not imagine from what it originated. I had eaten no fruit, caught no cold, and my breakfast was cold chicken and potatoes. My sufferings were intense;

at last I fainted when the train stopped. After I had recovered a little, the Consul General of Holland, who was in the train, and who kindly assisted me in my agony, asked me what I had eaten. As soon as I told him I had taken some Asti, he said that was the cause of my illness, and that it had the same effect upon all strangers, as it is badly fermented, and frequently the peasants put honey in to make it sweet. Therefore I warn all my readers never to drink Asti wine, and then journey in the cars.

Much weakened and fatigued, I arrived in Genoa, when, to my annoyance and sorrow, I found that the steamer for Civita Vecchia had not another berth, and that even the next steamer, which will start only in five days, is not certain to be able to accommodate us with berths. The season advances rapidly; the grapes will be picked in a few days in the south of France and in Spain; therefore I have resolved to leave Rome and Naples unvisited, as I can, through friends, order the cuttings and trees. This is all I can do for my readers and those who have engaged vines; for as to making wine as these people, God forbid! They are as far back in this art as are the Mission Indians in California. I have resolved to embark with the first steamer for Marseilles, and from there go on to Spain and Portugal, where I will be in season to see the curing of the raisins, which is very essential knowledge for California, as this will form a large profit to it.

September 10.—I went to engage my passage for Marseilles, and here again I met with difficulty about my passport; for, notwithstanding that it was viséd by the minister at Turin, it was necessary to have it viséd by the Consul at Genoa. I was obliged to submit, and took my passport to the Consul, Mr. Paterson, who received us cordially, and viséd it without charge. He is expecting his successor daily.

Before I leave Genoa I will add that this was the ancient seat of the pirates, who lived here in perfect security, accumulating immense wealth. To quiet their conscience, they put much of it in churches and church ornaments. There are a great many churches here, built of the most beautiful marble, having richly frescoed walls, and gold and silver vessels innumerable. Traces of magnificent palaces still exist. This place suffers much on account of our troubles. The people seem content with their present ruler, Victor Emanuel.

September 11.—At six o'clock this evening we embarked for Marseilles. During the night some wind arose, and when I went upon deck I found we were heading in for land. I inquired the reason of this movement, and whether we were to land at some port. The captain replied no. But as the wind continued to blow fresh, he ran the boat under shelter, and dropped anchor. The sky was clear, the day fine, but I thought that he might know certain signs which indicate a storm on this sea. We had anchored at the small village where Napoleon made his landing after escaping from Elba.

We lay there from eight o'clock A.M. till eight o'clock P.M. The wind was moderate, the weather clear; all the passengers, as well as myself, wondered why the captain did not raise anchor, when we had seen several large vessels pass us with sails full set. Still, I did not feel vexed, as my previous rapidity in traveling left me but little time to read my books upon wine, silk, etc., which I must finish, so as to be posted when I reach those countries where they are produced. I was quite at ease, as I thought that the captain had to board us until we land. In the evening the wind died away, and we started.

There were more than eighty steerage passengers, men, women, and children, all huddled together like so many swine. As these people had with them provisions only for twenty-four hours (in which time the steamer should make the trip), the poor children suffered a great deal.

September 12.—We arrived at half past twelve o'clock, but before we left the steamer the steward brought me a bill of twenty francs, and so to the other passengers, stating that the company gives us but two meals, a breakfast and dinner, and we had had one meal more. We objected, stating that we had asked when we paid sixty-two and a half francs apiece for our tickets, whether the board was included, and the officers replied that it was. Consequently, the company was obliged to board us; besides, there was no earthly reason for lying by, as the wind was not more than required for a sail-boat. Our arguments were vain, and, to avoid farther parley, we paid what was charged.

We did not disembark at a wharf, but were obliged to go ashore in a yawl. After waiting a long time in the custom-house for our baggage, it at last arrived. The officers politely passed it without opening the trunks.

Marseilles is a large, busy sea-port town. There are innumerable large, fine iron steamers in the inclosed harbor.

G

CHAPTER VII.

THE BORDEAUX WINE DISTRICT.

September 13.—At eight o'clock we started on our way to Bordeaux from Marseilles. From this city to Rognac the country is planted with olive-trees, vines, and almonds. The olive is predominant, and is of a dwarfish kind. The almond-trees are trimmed as dwarfs. Some part of the country is rocky. The vines are planted in two rows, about two feet apart, and these are separated from the next two by a space of about ten feet. From this place to St. Chamas the country was poor and rocky in the extreme, but, wherever there was a place to plant, were found almond, olive, and mulberry trees. To Miramas the lands are planted with olives, mixed much with mulberries. Silk is here raised in large quantities. To Arles the country is a large plain, very rocky, and almost a desert. No trees, no grass can there be seen ; all that meets the wearied eye is, from time to time, a sheep-house, but there are no sheep visible, as the scanty tufts of grass must be sought far and wide. The whole country has the aspect of an ancient river-bed. It is about twenty-five miles across. We afterward came to a region which was a little more fertile. It had now and then some olive and more mulberry trees, but hay was the principal product. We saw some well-loaded fruit-trees, and in the distance some mountains which exclusively produce fruit, almonds, and vines. Till Secoloux there were more or less mulberry-trees and vines. There was some grain, but the soil was very inferior, being of a poor gray color. At Talasco we changed cars. The land and cultivation are the same as above until Mandeuil.

Nismes.—To the right the country was rolling, and planted with mulberry-trees. There were many young plantations. The olive-trees extend for miles and miles. We now and then passed some almond-trees. On the left side the country was more planted with grain. There were, however, many mulberry and olive trees in the same fields, either in rows or on the edges. After passing the Rhone vines are almost exclusively planted. Sometimes there are olive or mulberry trees having vines between them, but the practice is not general. I saw a plow, by which land was subsoiled, drawn by five mules, at the last place. Wherever the soil was red, vines were cultivated. The table-land this side of Talasco, as far as the eye can reach, is planted with vines, olive-trees, and mulberry-trees.

Milhaud.—Plantations of vines, with olive-trees between. The species of vine is the blue grape.

Uchaud.—On the right-hand side are rolling, rocky, low hills, planted with vines and olives. On the left is a plain. It is well elevated, and planted with olive and mulberry trees. The vintage has already here begun, and goes on speedily.

Vergere.—On either side, for miles and miles, there extends a plain, planted with vines, olives, and some mulberry trees.

Galargues.—The land is similar in aspect to that above.

Lunel.—This place is famous for its sweet wine, which is made in the same way, and is the rival of Frontignan wine. The soil, wherever vines are planted, is red. Its aspect is the same as above.

We arrived at Montpellier, where we stopped to see the surrounding country and the method of here making wine. Immediately on our arrival we set out to visit the olive-presses. We staid here over night, and started at eight o'clock for Bordeaux.

Villeneuve.—There were vines on each side of us, and all cultivated in the same way as mine in California. There were few olives and mulberries.

Vice-Merval.—The valley has been getting narrower. We passed through vines and some meadows which were well loaded.

Frontignan.—The vines are here much loaded. This is the place where the famous Frontignan wine is made. There are two varieties of grapes in the vicinity, the red Muscat and the white Muscat, of which the latter is the most in cultivation. The vineyards generally give ten per cent. on the value of the land. An acre is estimated at from fifteen to twenty thousand francs.

Cette.—Here we changed cars, the ones we were in going to Perpignan. The railroad runs through shoals of the sea from Frontignan to Cette. Every where that a foot of ground can be redeemed from them, it is done, and the spot is planted with vines; these, all along the sea-coast, were doing excellently. Cette is the great manufacturing place for spurious wines, millions of gallons of imitations being here made, of every brand in existence, and sold to all parts of the world, a few drops of the genuine being used to give the taste of the different qualities. So perfect are some of these imitations, that it is with difficulty you can distinguish the spurious wines from the genuine. The country around being flat and the soil sandy, the wine is very poor, and, as the vines yield largely, the wine is almost as cheap as water. The manufacturers buy up these wines, and, by their chemical preparations, fix them up, and sell them, mostly to the American market, for good prices. Such are the wines we drink as Chateau Margaux, Lafitte, Chambertin, etc., etc.

Adge.—The vines were planted still nearer the shore, and were looking well.

Narbonne.—Here we breakfasted. The whole country is one wide plain, and planted with vines. The soil is of a grayish color.

Capendu.—The country reaching up to this place varies from a plain to rolling ground, and has on all sides vineyards. Now and then may be seen some olive and almond trees raised in hedges.

Carcassonne.—Some of the land is planted with grain; the principal part of it is still planted with vines, however. There are hundreds of acres which have been turned into vineyards since the last twenty-five years. It seems to pay better than any thing else, as there is an extreme demand for common wines, which are used to correct other wines wanting color, strength, or body.

Rames.—The vineyards diminish and almost disappear. Wheat is the principal product. The plowing is done by oxen.

Castelaundrey.—The land is cultivated with grain, and appears pretty rich. There is a great quantity of Indian corn raised. It is *topped* to the corn-ears.

Villefranche de Lauregais.—The valley is exclusively composed of farming lands. The hills on either side are planted with vines.

Toulouse.—We here caught the first sight of the great Canal de Midi. It did quite a good business formerly; but, since the inauguration of the railroad, its importance has much diminished. The vine is predominant.

Orisales.—The country is rolling; produces some wine and much corn.

Montlartier.—Vines on one side of the road, and grain, mixed with vines, on the other.

Montauban.—A large Protestant town, and famous in the history of the Huguenots. Vines are planted on each side of the road.

Castel-Sarrasin.—The vines are here planted in rows three feet apart, and these separated by a distance of forty to sixty feet, which is occupied by grain.

Marsac.—Vines are on either side of the track. The River Tarn flows along the valley.

Malouse.—The plum or prune cultivation begins to increase. On the hills, which are of moderate height, vines are planted. I saw many patches of cane, which is used for the drying of the plums.

Valence.—The country is cultivated with vines, grain, and fruit-trees.

St. Nicolas.—The cultivation is the same as above. The railroad runs for a length of time on the banks of the canal.

Agen.—A large place, famous for its dried plums, of which there are sometimes only thirty-six to a pound. After passing Agen night came on, and I could make no farther observations. We arrived at Bordeaux at twelve o'clock, well worn out with our day's journey.

September 15.—As it was Sunday, all that could be done was to walk around the city and write correspondence. Bordeaux is a very fine city. It possesses large shady walks, promenades, and squares. It has a good safe harbor in the River Garonne. Its botanic gardens, with their beautiful ponds, in which hundreds of gold-fish swim, and upon which swans extend their white and graceful forms, contribute in no small measure to the beauty of the city and the pleasure of the promenading community. Many ships from our own country sweep the harbor with their airy forms. High above all the others is unfurled to the winds the beautiful *Star-spangled Banner*. In beholding the flag of my country, I felt rush into my heart a thrill of pleasure and pride. Even without the flag, it was easy to recognize at once our American ships. Their high masts, towering far above the forest around them, their sharp-cut bows, their finely-moulded lines, pronounced them American.

I saw building in the harbor two iron gun-boats. The steel plates were being put on; they were five inches thick. These boats are meant for the protection of the harbor; they are anchored at the entrance, and defend its passage. There were also building men-of-war. Several were completed; they were all steel-plated. The stone bridge across the Garonne is a very fine work of art. Bordeaux possesses several fine public buildings, of which the theatre is the principal. It is the finest and largest in France. What is most remarkable in it is the architectural beauty of the interior.

September 16.—The first thing I did this morning was to visit the house of Mr. Alfred de Luze—the largest wine-dealing establishment in Bordeaux, as it also is the most recommendable one. Monsieur de Luze is also consul of Frankfort and of the Grand-duchy of Hesse. The stately old gentleman received us with great cordiality, offering his services for any information or letters of introduction that we might need. Offered in the gracious manner that it was, and coming from such a source, I of course accepted it with pleasure, well knowing that it would be the means of making a thorough investigation in this vicinity.

Before leaving the office, M. Francis de Luze, son and partner in the house, kindly invited us to visit the vaults. Accordingly, myself and my son Arpad followed our polite conductor. We came to the cooper's shop, where a dozen or more men were at work repairing the barrels. Good wine is never put into new barrels. It is a universal custom in Bordeaux, in well-conducted houses, to use for first quality wine barrels which have already contained wine, which has taken out the astringent taste of the wood. These barrels, however, are taken completely apart and thoroughly cleansed, piece by piece. The barrels which we saw were intended for shipment.

Leaving the shop, we entered the vaults. Going from one to the other, we saw each filled with wine-casks four and five tiers high. Our steps led us through vault after vault, and each successive one became larger. Some of these vaults had six to eight rows of barrels five to six tiers high. Rows, not against the walls, are composed of two barrels touching each other at one end, and having the other on a little alley which separates them from the next row. Mr. de Luze made us taste all the principal wines of the establishment. I need hardly say that they were delicious. Never had I before tasted such Bordeaux or Sauterne, though of each I had previously known excellent brands.

From this series of vaults we were taken through a series of smaller ones. They were narrow and long, being the place where the wine in bottles is kept. On each side the bottles are piled up to the roof, and each side is composed of one row four bottles deep. These vaults each contain several hundred thousand bottles, which have been here for many years awaiting their term of maturity. The contents of the cellars in bottles and barrels at the present time can not fall short of half a million of gallons. It took us two full hours to visit this grand establishment.

The custom of this house is only to buy in good years, and then largely. Last year being a bad one, no wine was bought except for the consumption of the laborers of the establishment.

The price of the wine depends upon the age and upon the year, coming from the same growth. The price of a barrel of sixty gallons is from 300 to 2000 francs, and sometimes even more. The bottled wines cost from three francs to eight francs apiece; but, of course, they are only sold at wholesale.

I am particular in describing this establishment, that my readers, who have flattered themselves that they have bought good Bordeaux in San Francisco at $40 and $50 a barrel, or at $4 to $5 a case, have been most egregiously deceived. Their Bordeaux was nothing more nor less than a miserable imitation. No good wine can be sold even here at any such price. Where, then, is the cost of transportation, insurance, interest, and duty, to say nothing of profits?

I may here mention the curious fact that this family has carried on the wine trade during four generations. This is very singular to us Americans, who change business so often in life, and sometimes in a year.

When we had seen every thing, and tasted all the noble wines, we took our leave, not, however, before receiving and accepting an invitation to dinner the next day, and a drive in the environs. After leaving Alfred de Luze's establishment, we visited several other manufactories of little importance; among these was one which makes the capsules to place on the cork, and stamps them. The capsules, all stamped, cost twenty francs a thousand.

Making the necessary arrangements for to-morrow's work, we afterward went to dinner, then wrote, and then went to bed.

September 17.—At seven o'clock, according to appointment, Francis de Luze called with his carriage. We drove out several miles from Bordeaux, inspecting the vineyards, orchards, barrel manufactories, etc., etc. I was informed by M. de Luze that the barrels meant to contain fine Cognacs were made from Russian oak. The reason given for this is, that other wood gives an unpleasant taste to the brandy. New barrels made from Russian oak, holding sixty American gallons, having four iron hoops and the rest wooden, cost from twenty to twenty-two francs.

Leaving the cooper's shop, we drove to the largest nursery at Bordeaux, where M. de Luze left us. We examined this extensive establishment, and made our selections in fruit-trees from the fruit which we saw. We here found the very nicest and finest fruit that we had yet seen in France. After making and completing my contract with M. Catros-Gerand, I went home to complete my journal and write up my correspondence. On our way home we saw a bird-fancier who had some very fine pheasants, and a large variety of very rare birds. He asked sixty francs a pair for his pheasants, and ten francs for some fine pigeons. I was really sorry that I was not on my way home, else I would have bought the pheasants and other rare fowls.

In the afternoon we were taken by a nephew of M. de Luze to the establishment of A. Dufour & Co., whose business consists in packing and putting up dried prunes for exportation. We were politely shown round by the proprietor, and visited the whole establishment. It is situated in a large five-story house, each story having its special operation. The prunes, after having been bought from the producers, have again to be prepared by drying; for, to make them weigh more and appear larger, the producers do not dry them thoroughly. This operation is repeated only when the prunes are destined for distant lands and for long keeping. When they are not sent from France they may be put up as they are, after the selections have been made. The largest and best prunes are put into glass jars; the second best are put into paper boxes tastily prepared. Our guide showed us boxes thus prepared which were to be sent to Havana, the box itself costing twenty sous, while the prunes in it only cost eleven sous.

Thus the good people of Havana pay thirty-one sous for what they might have had for eleven. See where a taste for pretty things leads people. There is a still cheaper box which goes to the United States. The third sort goes in tin boxes, round or square. The fourth sort is put into barrels, and is meant for home consumption. Great system is employed in the whole matter. The house now employs eighty-five women and twelve men. Before the war in the United States broke out it employed two hundred and eighty women and thirty-five men. There are many other establishments in this vicinity which are fully as large as the above.

Many of my readers will be astonished at the magnitude of this trade; I myself was surprised at its great extent. I knew before that it was carried on on a large scale here, in Hungary, and in Germany, but I never dreamed that it was so extensive.

Why do not we Californians and brother planters try this trade? Our soil is much richer than that of Europe, and the method of drying the prunes is comparatively easy. We might, with the greatest ease, furnish all America, North and South. Why bring our goods from afar when we can procure them at home? When I have thoroughly made my investigation, I will give, at some future day, the modes of preparing these prunes as practiced here and in other parts of Europe.

Having fully investigated this house, we went to the chateau of M. de Luze. It is within half an hour's walk from his office. The chateau is an old family residence, lately repaired and ornamented under the direction of the old gentleman, who prides himself on such things, and displays very good taste. Surrounding it is a very fine park, which procures him all the pleasures of a country residence. The furniture of the chateau is all in the style of Louis XIV. and Louis XV., and is in the very best taste. We had a very good dinner, and a still better wine. We were here again made to drink of all the best years and of the best growths. The old gentleman lives in an elegant style, showing that the wine business is much better, in way of revenue, than that of many ducal estates. We left our kind host late in the evening. To-morrow we will visit Chateau Margaux.

September 18.—This morning we hired a carriage, and, accompanied by M. de Luze's nephew, we went to see the wine country. We stopped at the village of Margaux, about eighteen miles from Bordeaux. This is the wine district which has the greatest reputation in all France. It is here that the renowned "Chateau Margaux" is made. The soil is gravelly, and intermixed with a great quantity of pebbles. It is of a gray color, some clay, but more sand. The grapes near the village are small and blue. The vines are kept low, being on trellis-work only two feet high. They are three feet apart each way. The vines are nearly all sulphured. The *oïdium* rages here. The frost in the beginning of the spring did much harm.

After having breakfasted we went to the Chateau Margaux, which is on the borders of the village. It consists of about eighty hectares, and belongs to the Marquis Aguado. The *regisseur* reluctantly gave his consent to us to see the place. However, he sent us to the head cooper, who was to show us around. We entered a long room, supported by pillars in the centre. There were but a few barrels here. In bad years it is here that the wine is kept. In good years the wine is sold immediately upon coming from the tanks or fermenting-tubs, or but a short time afterward. The country being all flat and near the river, no cellars are made. We were led into the room where the wine in bottles is kept. It is about sixty feet long, narrow, and very well arranged to pile up bottles. The divisions are of stone, and each contains about 200 bottles.

The press-house is also very well arranged. There are seventeen large fermenting-tubs on one side of the room. The other contains four large stone vats, one foot deep and twelve feet square. In the middle of two of these there are two round presses. The sides of these are composed of perpendicular slats two to three inches wide, and as many thick. They are placed wide enough apart to let out the juice, but not the seeds and skins. In the centre is an iron screw, which is worked from above.

The grapes, when brought from the vineyard, are thrown upon tables whose bottoms are made of slats crossing each other at right angles, and permitting the grapes to pass between. As soon as they are on these tables, the workmen, with the flat of the hand, rub them against the bottom. The berries by this operation fall through the slats, and the stem remains. It is immediately picked out and thrown in a tub placed for that purpose.

The fermentation lasts from seven to ten days. Then the wine is taken off, the residue put into the press and pressed. This forms the second quality wine. When the second quality has been made, the matter pressed is again thrown into a large fermenting-tub and fermented, after water has been poured upon it. This latter wine forms the drink of the workmen of the establishment. There are about 400 barrels made per annum.

We visited one more domain, Chateau Rauzan, with its vineyards, presses, etc. It was about the same thing as the former, with the exception that the tanks were not in such good order, and that the slatted tables were over the fermenting-tubs instead of on the tanks. The grapes are thrown upon the tables by shovels. When rubbed from the stems then fall into the fermenting-tubs, where they are stamped by men. The rest of the wine-making establishments are conducted in nearly the same way.

I was really astonished how they could make any wine at all, the vines were so much affected by disease. Sulphuring must be very costly. Many vineyards will not make a single barrel of wine this year for the reason which I have already stated, that the frost killed nearly all the vines in the beginning of spring. The whole district of *Cognac* will not this year produce ten barrels. The proprietors, however, take it very coolly, saying that they will make it all up next year.

The land lying between Chateau Margaux and Bordeaux is in many parts sandy, and large tracts lay idle, not even producing grain. Other parts of these sandy tracts are planted with pitch pine. The older parts of these plantations yield turpentine. We returned in the evening much fatigued.

The following extract from Victor Rendu's *Ampelographie Française* will give a more correct idea to the reader of the country and its wines:

THE WINES OF BORDEAUX.

The wines bearing the general appellation of Bordeaux wines, because they grow in the country surrounding this celebrated emporium, and are shipped to all parts of the world from its harbor, are divided into four principal classes:

1. *Vins de Medoc.*—Wines of the Medoc district. Of these we shall treat in detail hereafter.

2. *Vins de Grave.*—Wines growing on the gravelly soil in the immediate neighborhood of Bordeaux, and on both sides of the rivers Dordogne and Garonne, within a certain distance of their confluence.*

* Of the red wines grown on this soil the most renowned are those of Chateau Haut-Brion. Of much less note are the wines of Merignac, Carbonnieux, and Leognan. Among the white wines the most popular are the Sauternes, the Barsac, the Preignac, and the Bommes. Again, among these, the most superior is the white wine of Chateau Iquem, in the parish of Sauterne, which has been sold up to 1200 francs per tun.

3. *Vins des Côtes.*—Wines growing on the range of hills at the right side of the Garonne, from Ambares to Saint Croix du Mont. Also on the right side of the Dordogne, between Bourg and Fronsac. Of these wines, the most celebrated are those of St. Emilion. Less choice are those of St. Laurent, St. Hippolyte, St. Christophe de St. Georges, and of Pommerol. The soil in these vineyards is generally a combination of lime and clay, with a subsoil of hard rock. They generally decline toward south and west.

4. *Vins de Palus.*—Wines growing on the bottom-lands of the Garonne, near Bordeaux. These are less distinguished than the above, although they are wines of a fine color and a good deal of spirit. The best of them are grown in the communes of Queyries and Montferrand.

Wines of the Medoc District.

The small peninsula formed by the River Gironde on its eastern side and the Atlantic on the western, is generally allowed to contain some of the finest vineyards in the world. This is the renowned Medoc district. It offers itself to the eye as a softly-undulating plain, with gentle declivities all along the river, and sandy downs, frequently interrupted by marshes and lagoons, along the sea-side. It is principally on those slopes above the Gironde where the famous Bordeaux wines are raised in their greatest perfection. The general formation of the soil consists here of a compound of quartzose fragments with clay, strongly impregnated with oxide of iron. This uppermost stratum rests either on a bed of pure sand, or on a conglomerate of gravel with clay, and a strong admixture of iron oxide, which composition—very hard in some cases, and soft and crumbling in others—goes by the local name of "alios."

This diversity of the soil, or, rather, the great variation in the mixture of its component elements, is the principal cause for the great diversity of its productions. As a proof of this, we find, in many instances, wines of inferior quality in the close neighborhood of the very best vineyards, and, *vice versâ*, streaks of good soil amid poor vineyards, giving a much better wine than the surrounding grounds. The culture of the vine in the Medoc district varies more or less from the methods used in other parts of France; but the training of the vines on laths or on trellises near the ground is a characteristic not to be found any where else but here.

The most extensively cultivated grapes in the Medoc are the Cabernet-Sauvignon, the Franc-Cabernet, the Meilot, the Malbec, and the Verdot; but it is especially the Cabernet-Sauvignon which forms the basis of the Medoc vineyards, and, in fact, is to the great Medoc wines what the Pineau is to the wines of the Côte d'Or in Burgundy. This unsurpassed grape is the chief ingredient of the celebrated wines of Panillac, St. Julien, and Margaux; and about five eighths of the plantations of Lafitte, Mouton, Latour, Leoville, Margaux, Rauzan, etc., belong to the same. The wine made of it is of a splendid color and an exquisite bouquet. A little tart at the beginning, it requires to be kept in wood for four years, and then for two in the bottle, to arrive to its full maturity. It gains in excellence up to its fifteenth year, and preserves all its qualities till the twentieth; beyond this it loses gradually some of its smoothness, and becomes more and more dry.

' The method of cultivation is uniform all through the Medoc district, and does not present any striking difference from the methods pursued in other parts of France. The vines are generally planted from April to June. The distance observed is one metre and ten centimetres between the vines on one and the same line, and only one metre between the rows. In the second year the vine is pruned to two or three eyes; in the third it begins to be trained on a trellis by tying two sprigs, each with two or three eyes, to the lath. The pruning commences usually in November and lasts till January.

In the Medoc district the vine is in blossom in the middle of June, and the grape ripens, in favorable years, about the middle of September. In such years the vintage begins on the 20th of September and lasts to the 1st of October. If it takes place altogether in this month, the year is pronounced to be middling or bad. Every body may gather his grapes when he pleases, as there is no time fixed by statute for this purpose in the Department of the Gironde, to which the Medoc district belongs.

The grapes are carefully picked, and cleaned of green or rotten berries before they are taken to the press-room. Here the wine-presses stand, generally three of them, ranged on one side, and the vats along the opposite wall. The berries are all plucked from their stalks, which is done either with rakes or an instrument called an *egrappoir*. After this they are trodden down in tubs, which generally have a hole in the bottom through which the must escapes. This is taken to the vat, which is scrupulously cleaned and sponged with brandy. The vat being once full, must be left perfectly quiet until the wine is formed, which may take some four or five days, or even longer, according to the temperature, weather, ripeness of the grapes, etc. As soon as the must has lost its sugary taste, and has turned fairly into wine, it is drawn carefully into casks, during which operation great care is taken not to let any foreign matter be mixed with the pure juice of the grape. The filling of the casks must be done as quick as possible. During the first month they must be filled up every four or five days; the second month, once in eight days; and subsequently once in fifteen, until the wine is drawn off. This has to be done three times during the first year, viz., in January or February, in June, and in September. In the following years it is sufficient to draw off only twice. Ordinarily, the Medoc wines are

left four years in the cask before they are bottled; and in two
years more they will be perfectly mellow and ready for the market.

The Medoc district contains about 20,000 hectares of wine-land.
The average produce is at the rate of two tuns (say 18 hectolitres and 24 litres) per hectare, amounting in all to 40,000 tuns.
Of this quantity about 4500 belong to the first class wines, an
equal quantity to the second but still superior class, and the balance to ordinary wines.

The superior wines of the Medoc are classified in the Bordeaux
commerce into five different qualities. The first class contains
only three wines, which are ranged as follows:

1. Chateau Margaux, 100–110 tuns per year.
2. Chateau Lafitte, 120–150 tuns per year.
3. Chateau Latour, 70–90 tuns per year.

The vineyard of Chateau Margaux contains 80 hectares. The
soil consists of a gray gravel, with a substratum of "alios." The
greater part of the vineyard looks toward east and west, but the
best part of it inclines to south and north. The Cabernet-Sauvignon vine occupies about one half of this celebrated vineyard.
In a first-rate year the wine of Chateau Margaux surpasses by far
every other Bordeaux wine, even Lafitte and Latour not excepted;
but in less favorable years these two wines are superior to their
great rival. The chemical composition of the soil of this famous
vineyard is as follows:

Oxide of iron	3.341
Alumina	1.590
Magnesia	0.263
Soluble silicates	0.380
Phosphoric acid	0.147
Potash	1.291
Carbonate of lime	0.891
Organic matter	6.670
Insoluble residue	85.427
	100.000

The vineyard of Chateau Lafitte contains 47 hectares. Its situation is various, but mostly northerly. The soil, and especially
the subsoil, is very rich in quartz pebbles. Chateau Latour contains only 42 hectares. Its soil is very gravelly, and inclines
mostly toward south and north.

The second class of Medoc wines comprises the following vineyards:

	hectares		tuns per annum		
De Branno-Cantenac	45 hectares,	50 to	60	tuns per annum.	
Cos-Destournel	28 "	60 "	70 "	"	"
Duport de Vivens	32 "	30 "	35 "	"	"
Gruaud-Larosse	51 "	100 "	120 "	"	"
Lascombe	21 "	15 "	20 "	"	"
Leoville { Lascases	65 "	80 "	100 "	"	"
Leoville { Poyferé	30 "	40 "	50 "	"	"
Leoville { Barton	25 "	25 "	70 "	"	"
Mouton Rothschild	52 "	120 "	140 "	"	"
Prichon de Longueville	50 "	100 "	120 "	"	"
Rauzan-Rauzan	51 "	70 "	80 "	"	"

To the third class belong the following vineyards:

Issan	43 hectares,	50	to	70	tuns per annum.		
Desmirail	14 "	30	"	40	"	"	"
Philippe-Dubignon	13 "	15	"	20	"	"	"
Beau-Caillon	35 "	100	"	120	"	"	"
Fruitier	38 "	60	"	70	"	"	"
Ganot	16 "	20	"	25	"	"	"
Giscourt	45 "	80	"	100	"	"	"
Kirwan	24 "	35	"	40	"	"	"
Lagrange	122 "	120	"	150	"	"	"
Langod-Barton	70 "	100	"	120	"	"	"
Pouget et Chavaille	11 "	25	"	30	"	"	"
Lacotonie et Malescot	50 "	70			"	"	"

In the fourth class are reckoned   '

Talbot	69 hectares,	70	to	80	tuns per annum.		
Beycherelle	40 "	100	"	120	"	"	"
Calon-Lestapis	55 "	120	"	160	"	"	"
Carnet	52 "	100	"	120	"	"	"
Casteja, or Milon	30 "	60	"	70	"	"	"
Dubignon		12	"	15	"	"	"
Duluc, aine	60 "	80	"	90	"	"	"
Verrieres	8 "	10	"	15	"	"	"
Rochet	22 "	30	"	40	"	"	"
La Lagune	36 "	40	"	50	"	"	"
Solberg	30 "	25	"	30	"	"	"
Pagès au Prieure	11 "	25	"	30	"	"	"
Palmer	85 "	50	"	60	"	"	"
	18 "						
St. Pierre {	9 " }	50	"	70	"	"	"
	9 "						

Lastly, the fifth class contains, among others,

Batailly	34 hectares,	60	to	80	tuns per annum.		
De Bedout	17 "	50	"	55	"	"	"
Caneu.¹ outet	67 "	100	"	120	"	"	"
Cantemerle	91 "	120	"	130	"	"	"
Jurine	40 "	100	"	120	"	"	"
Ducasse	33 "	80	"	90	"	"	"
Le Grand Puy	52 "	50	"	60	"	"	"
Montpelouss-Casteja	14 "	25	"	30	"	"	"

The prices of all these wines vary, of course, according to the years and the demand. They arrived at their maximum in 1844, when Lafitte was sold at 4500 francs the tun, Haut-Brion at 3000, Mouton at 2500, Lagrange at 1900, Kirwan at 1850, Giscourt at 1800, Langod-Barton at 1600. In ordinary years the second quality wines are sold at from 1200 francs to 1400 francs the tun; the third quality at from 800 to 1000; the fourth for only little less; and the fifth, on an average, at 600 to 700. The first quality of Chateau Margaux have been contracted for nine years at the price of 2100 francs per tun, but the princely Chateau Lafitte generally sells at a much higher rate. Of the inferior wines, the better class (*Bourgeois superieurs*) are worth 400 to 500 francs a tun; the second class (*Bourgeois ordinaires*), 350 to 400; and the third (*Paysans*), 300 to 325 francs.

The best customers for the Medoc wines are the English, the

Dutch, and the Russians. Those exported to England are generally qualified for the British palate by being mixed with stronger
wines, and especially with the red wines of the Ermitage district.

M. Franck, who has published an elaborate work on the great
Bordeaux wines, quotes the following prices at which some vineyards of the Medoc have changed hands.

Chateau Margaux (80 hectares), bought, in 1804, for 651,000,
was sold in 1836 to M. Aguado for 1,300,000 francs.

Malescot (Margaux), in 1853, for 280,000 francs.

Gruaud-Larosse (St. Julien, 51 hectares), in 1814, for 350,000
francs.

Langon (St. Julien, 40 hectares), in 1851, for 650,000 francs.

Beycherelle (St. Julien, 40 hectares), for 650,000 francs.

La Grange (St. Julien, 122 hectares), in 1832, for 650,000 francs;
in 1842, for 775,000 francs.

Lafitte (Panillac, 67 hectares), in 1803, for 1,200,000 francs.

Mouton (25 hectares), bought, in 1853, by M. Rothschild for
1,125,000 francs.

Baye, for 300,000 francs.

Batailly (34 hectares), for 150,000 francs.

Calon (St. Estèphe, 55 hectares), for 600,000 francs.

Du Bosq (St. Estèphe), for 190,000 francs.

Chateau d'Issan (Cantenac, 43 hectares), sold, in 1825, for
255,000 francs, was, in 1859, adjudged to the heirs of the Blanchy
estate for 470,000 francs.

Lacheney (Cussac), for 150,000 francs.

Laujac (Bégadan), for 400,000 francs.

Haut-Brion (Persac), for 525,000 francs.

Giscourt (Labarde, 45 hectares), for 500,000 francs.

Cos-d'Estournel (St. Estèphe, 28 hectares), for 1,150,000 francs.

Palmer (Cantenac, 85 hectares), for 425,000 francs.

Chateau d'Agarsac (Ludon), for 891,000 francs.

The same author, speaking of the Champagne and its wines,
says:

The wine-growing country of the Champagne district may be
properly divided into two topographical arteries: First, the hills
on the River Marne; and, second, the mountain of Rheims. The
first is again ramified into three different ranges: 1. The northern
side of the river, with the hill-sides looking due south, and to which
belong the distinguished vineyards of Hautvillers, Disy, Ay, and
Mareuil. 2. The opposite side of the river, which includes the
vineyards of Epernay, of Moussy, Pierry, and Vinay. 3. The range
of Avize, running in a southeasterly direction, parallel with the
côte of Epernay, and containing the vineyards of Cramant, Avize,
Oger, Mesnil, and Vertus.

The second general division of this great wine-district embraces
all the vineyards in the environs of Rheims, and is subdivided
into two zones: 1. The hilly part, containing Verzy, Verzenay,

Sillery, Mailly, Londes, Chigny, and Rilly; 2. The flat zone, with St. Thierry, Marsilly, Hermonville, and others. Besides these there is a small intermediate tract between the plain and the mountain, where the gentle declivities of Bouzy and of Ambonnay are to be found.

Most of the noted vineyards of the Champagne are situated on a formation of limestone and chalk, covered by a generally very superficial structure of vegetable mould. The soil may be said to contain fully four fifths of carbonate of lime, and only one fifth of clay, silicious and other matter. Oxide of iron also enters into its composition in several instances.

The vines mostly cultivated belong to the family of the Pineau, and generally bear dark grapes. They vary, however, to some extent from the original Pineau (or Pinot) of the Burgundy district, probably on account of the diversity of the soil in these wine-districts.

The cultivation of the vineyards is nearly uniform through all the province, but it may be said that at Ay it has been brought to its highest perfection. December is the best month for plantation, although it may be continued even to the end of March. The ground is always manured at the time of planting. The young plant, generally a rooted vine two or three years old, is dug round four times during the first year. In the second year it is pruned down to one or two eyes, according to the vigor of the plant, and the soil is worked up again four times in the course of the year. In the third year a certain proportion of the most vigorous plants are used. When in bearing order the vine is generally kept low, and tied to a stick.

The vines are in blossom about St. John's Day, and are carefully freed from all new sprouts (*gourmands*) after this time. The grapes arrive at their full ripeness in September, and the vintage begins, in favorable years, in the middle of this month; in less favorable ones at the beginning of October; and in bad years not before the middle of the same month. Every body is at liberty to gather his grapes when he pleases. The grapes are carefully picked by women, and cleaned on the spot from all spoiled berries, leaves, etc. Then they are carefully selected according to their ripeness and perfection, and sent to the press-house.

The manufacture of wine has been raised to the proportions of a particular art or science in the Champagne district during the last fifty years, and forms a special industry, frequently entirely separated from the culture of the vine. Nearly all the wine produced in this district is made into sparkling wine; and the formerly celebrated brands of dry Champagne wines—namely, the red wines of Sillery, of Bouzy, Verzenay, and Mailly—scarcely exist any more in commerce. The same black grape which was the mother of these dark wines yields at present the juice for the pale wine, which, in its sparkling state, ranks uppermost in the estima-

H

tion of the wine-consuming public.   In some vineyards in this district, however, white grapes are planted in preference to the black ones, and it has been ascertained that if judiciously mixed (say one eighth to one quarter of white, the balance of black grapes), they add to the excellence of the wine, made into sparkling Champagne.

The grapes must be passed very rapidly through the wine-press, to avoid all fermentation in the berries, and all coloring of the must.   The must is not immediately barreled, but left for from twelve to twenty-four hours in vats, so that it may deposit all its coarser dregs; then it is drawn into scrupulously cleaned and sulphured barrels.   In these the wine generally ferments until Christmas.   If rich in sugar, this fermentation will progress very slowly, and will be the more rapid the less sugary particles the must contains.   In the second half of December the wine is drawn off for the first time, without taking any notice of the particular state of the atmosphere.   Now is the time to test the quality of the wines, and to mix the different qualities, or, in some cases, wines of different vineyards and localities judiciously together, so as to obtain the most perfect mixture.   After this operation the wine is cleared with gelatine, and then drawn off again through a double sieve of hair and silk which is placed on the funnel.   By this the entrance of all foreign matter will be avoided.   Generally, very little gelatine is used; but in most cases a little tannin in the liquid state is added to the wine as a preservative against various maladies.   In this condition the wine remains till the month of April, when it is drawn off again for the purpose of being manufactured into sparkling Champagne.*

The white wines of Champagne are classified into the "Great Sparkling Wine," *Grand Mousseux;* the "Ordinary Sparkling Wine," *Mousseux ordinaire;* the "Half Sparkling Wine," *Demi-Mousseux,* or *Crémant;* the "Non-sparkling," or "dry" Champagne, *Non Mousseux;* and a very light, weak, sweet, and slightly sparkling quality, called *Tisane de Champagne.*   The sparkling wines attain their full maturity in the third year after being bottled, and will lose nothing of their sparkling quality within a dozen years.   The half sparkling wine, if of a good source, is considered by connoisseurs as the king of all white Champagne wines.

In first-rate years the Champagne district will produce not less than fifteen million bottles of white wine, and the average production may be rated at seven millions per annum.   This commerce has been rapidly increasing for about forty years.   The principal markets for it are England, Germany, and Russia; and the names of the great manufacturers, Moët, Cliquot, Ruinart, Roederer, Piper, Perier, Dinot, are well known all over the world.

Having completed our observations on the famous wine district of Bordeaux, we prepared to take our departure for Spain.

* A minute description of the *modus operandi* in the most renowned factories of the Champagne district is given in another part of this work.

CHAPTER VIII.

JOURNEY THROUGH SPAIN: WINE, RAISINS, AND OLIVES.

Departure for Spain.—Delay for Passports.—Country between Bordeaux and Bay-
onne.—Shepherds on Stilts.—Bayonne.—Loading Revolvers.—Napoleon at
Hand.—Start by Diligence for Madrid.—The Diligence.—The Driver and the
Mules.—The Postillion.—On Spanish Frontier.—Ascent of the Pyrenees.—Des-
olate Aspect of the Country.—Breakfast.—Water and Towel.—Another Inspec-
tion of Baggage.—A Municipal Misunderstanding.—Burgos.—The Railway.—
Passengers bound for a Bull-fight.—Delay.—Train full.—Passengers left behind.
—Change Cars.—Delay again.—Refreshments.—Arrival at Madrid.—Our Hotel.
—Compassionate Waiter.—The Fair.—The Royal Palace.—The Prado.—The
Fountain.—General Description of the Country traversed.—Product.—Execrable
Wines.—Leave Madrid for Malaga.—Delay.—Difficulty about Baggage.—Final-
ly settled.—Off at last.—Stopped again.—One Passenger too many.—A Discus-
sion.—The extra Child.—A Night Ride.—Morning.—Beggars.—Vines appear.
—Ordinary Spanish Wines very poor.—The Boy again.—Building a Railway.—
Barren Country.—A beautiful Valley.—Dinner at Victoria.—Arrival at Granada.
—See the City.—Our Carriage.—The Sights of Granada.—Beggars.—Start for
Malaga.—Notes by the Way.—Malaga.—Wine and Raisins.—Making Raisins.—
The Drying-grounds.—Picking and Packing.—Malaga Wines.—Vinegar-making.
—Fig Culture.—Horse-fight.—Apprehensions of Damages.—Manufacture of Ol-
ive Oil.—Cotton and Iron Manufactories.—Buy Plants.—Goat-milk.—Passports
again.—Depart for Alicante.—Aspect of the Coast.—Alicante.—Barcelona.—
Wine-making.—Leave for Paris, *via* Marseilles and Lyons.—Arrival at Paris.—
Give up Project of visiting Greece and Egypt.—Start for Home, *via* England.—
Arrive in America.

September 19.—We were very much annoyed by the trouble
we had in getting our passports viséd. Our consul shuts up his
office at three o'clock, and if an unfortunate American should not
arrive at that hour, no matter who he be, there is an end of it,
he has to wait twenty-four hours longer, for none of the other
consuls will visé his passport before seeing that of the American
consul. At eleven o'clock we went to our consul's office, but
found him absent. The lad in attendance told us that he was
maybe sick, and at his house. We persuaded the lad to stamp
our passports, that we might afterward take them to the consul
and have them signed. This he did, and then asked us for eleven
and a half francs, which is more than we had ever given. We
went to the consul's house, where, after knocking and ringing violently, the door was opened by some invisible hand; we walked

into a hall and through several empty rooms; at last we discovered a little girl, who was the consul's daughter. She informed us that her father had left for his office in the morning; that if he was not there she did not know where he was. This was very disagreeable news to us; for, had it not been for our passports, we could have started at six o'clock in the morning, but we were delayed by this for the two o'clock train, and, from all appearance, would be liable even to miss that, and be left here over-night. This was uselessly wasting time, which was most precious to me, to say nothing of extra expenses. Returning to the office, and not finding the consul, I suggested to the lad to sign it himself, and state the absence of the consul. This was not legal, nor had the boy any authority whatever to do it; but, thinking the whole affair a *fuss*, and that the principal part was passed—namely, of taking the eleven and a half francs, I saw no harm in making the *fuss* bigger. The lad, after some hesitation, signed; we then proceeded to the Spanish consul, who, after stamping and signing, asked us for ten francs. We arrived just in time for the cars.

We were traveling eight hours from Bordeaux to Bayonne, and a more desolate and dreary country I have not seen since my arrival in Europe. It consists of immense plains, which are sandy, and only now and then possessing some pitch pine. Even these trees are of recent plantation. They are employed in making turpentine. These *landes*, as they are called, produce a kind of chapparal, but it is only from a foot to eighteen inches high. On these plains there are now and then seen some miserable sheep, guarded by men or women on stilts. As their flesh is so poor, what must their wool be? They resemble very much our Mexican sheep, only they are not so large nor so good-looking. But of all that is here seen, it is the stilts of the shepherds that is most noteworthy: they are from four to five feet high, and their owners remain on them the whole day without getting down. From this height they are better able to see their sheep in the bushes, and walk through the mud when there is any.

We arrived at the hotel at ten o'clock, and soon turned in.

Sept. 20. *Bayonne.*—In the morning we took a walk through the city. We visited its monuments and markets; in the latter the vegetables were very fine, and the grapes good and sweet. We ascertained that very little wine was raised in this vicinity.

In the River Gave, which runs through Bayonne, were anchored several large vessels. The two parts of the town are joined by a very fine bridge, newly built. The fortifications that lie on both sides of the river seem quite strong. After exchanging our money for Spanish coin, we went and engaged our places in the diligence office for the capital. Here we learned that the stage was to leave at six o'clock. Among several other items of disagreeable news, we were informed that it would take two nights and two days to reach Madrid, and, what was as bad, very little time was allowed to us for our meals. Besides this, we were told by every one whom we questioned that the roads were bad.

At ten o'clock a most sumptuous breakfast was served up. It by far surpassed many of our holiday dinners at home, if not in cooking, at least in variety.

After breakfast I wrote up my journal, some correspondence, then set out in search of a gunsmith to load my Colt's revolver, for I feared that I might have some use for it in Spain. The ticket-seller told me that it was pretty safe; but, as I read on my ticket, "*The Company is not responsible for any effects taken by armed force*," I thought "discretion the better part of valor," and had my pistol well loaded. With an eight-inch "Colt," I thought I might meet on pretty equal terms quite a considerable "armed force."

The Emperor Napoleon is at this moment in the bathing-place of Biarritz, about twenty minutes' drive from here. To-day he is expected to pass by Bayonne on his return to Paris, and all along where he is to pass the road is decorated with flags, flowers, garlands, and arches of triumph. Great enthusiasm is every where shown, and, from all I here saw, he is very much loved in this part of France.

Precisely at six in the evening we started with the diligence. There were about twenty passengers, and a quantity of large trunks, some of which would hold the whole household furniture of six families living out West. Besides these immense trunks there were several dry-good boxes belonging to some merchant passenger, which attained still greater dimensions. With all this weight, the six powerful horses hitched to our diligence took us along at a good sharp rate. At the first station we again took six horses. When I speak of a diligence, let not my readers imagine an American stage; it differs in every respect.

The wheels are large and heavy; the box, which is painted in a tasty manner, is divided into four divisions, each having its own entry and its own price. These divisions, naming them by the order of their rank and price, are the *Berline, Interieur, Rotonde,* and *Coupé*. In the Berline there are three places, all fronting the horses, having each a window in front, and the two side places one on the side. After the Berline, which is in the front of the diligence, comes the Interieur. It has six places, three toward the front and three opposite. The four side places have each a window. Like the Berline, the Interieur has two entries, one on each side. The Rotonde possesses four places, two on each side of the carriage, and parallel to it. Behind each place there is a window, and the entry is from behind. In front, on a level with the top of the diligence, is the driver's seat. Right behind this is the Coupé. It has four places, one for the conductor, and three for passengers. It is covered by a thick covering of leather, of the exact shape of an old American buggy. Behind this was the roof of the diligence, on which the baggage was put; and, after being firmly lashed on, covered over with a thick covering of leather. Sometimes it happens that all the space under this covering is not taken up by the baggage; it is then used to stow away passengers who travel as fifth class. The only light, the only air these poor fellows get, steals itself through the little hole behind the conductor's seat, which also serves as door. They have not even a bench to sit upon. It is useless to say that this is the cheapest place. The Coupé, in price, comes after the Rotonde. We chose our seats in the Coupé. At the end of our journey, far from repenting of our choice, we found that it was a most happy one; for, while the other passengers were half suffocated from dust and the want of air, we suffered from neither. The only objection of our seats was the difficulty to get out and in: this difficulty was much heightened by a woman who had a child in her lap, and who occupied the third place in the Coupé.

At the next station they hitched on thirteen mules, and away we went, full gallop up and down hill, the driver hallooing, shouting, yelling, and cracking his whip. His yells would have done honor to an American savage. What, however, most astonished me was the driver's descending and mounting to his seat while the mules were in full gallop. It was at least ten feet above the ground. When his mules would not pay any more attention to the cracks of his whip or to his voice, he would quietly descend, and, after whipping them from the last to the first rank, all the while uttering the most unearthly sounds, he would climb quietly up to his seat again, although the whole equipage might be on a full run. No sooner would he be in his seat than he would recommence his yells, and ply his whip most vigorously. There is on the leading mule or horse a postillion, whose only duty is to halloo to wagons and carts which are met to turn out of the road. It is a curious sight thus to see twelve to sixteen mules, in two or in three rows, going along with all their speed, the two last only having lines, the others tied one to another by their halter-strings. The postillion has a control only over his own mule and the one beside it. Such a scene is as hard to describe as it is curious. Although the postillion only controls the first two mules, and the driver the last two, they dash away at the greatest speed, plying their whips, shouting, yelling, bawling. When the driver gets down to whip the mules, the conductor takes his place, whips unmercifully all those he can reach, and screams at those he can not reach. When an unaccustomed traveler sees himself carried along at such a rate, on the brink of precipices from two hundred to six hundred feet, by twelve to sixteen mules without reins, he involuntarily shuts his eyes, and recommends his soul to its Maker.

We arrived at about ten o'clock in the evening at a place where we were asked for our passports by the French authorities, who scarcely gave them a glance. We crossed a bridge and were in Spanish territory. Here we got out to have our baggage thoroughly examined, as well as our passports, by the Spanish authorities. For having the latter again viséd we were obliged to pay once more. We might have dispensed with their visé, but they could not have done without our *reals*, for they were a most hungry-looking set.

After uselessly spending two hours here, we resumed our course, drawn on by sixteen mules. It was a fine moonlight night, and I could see the country all around. We were ascending the Pyrenees. In the ravines was planted Indian corn. The hills are barren, and have few, if even any trees on them. Soon it began to rain, and I could no longer see out. At twelve o'clock we arrived at St. Sebastien, where we were nearly upset in trying to get through a gate. The string of mules was so long that they could not give the proper turn, and the gate was so narrow that we ran up against one of the posts. At last, after a few moments of hallooing and whipping, we got through. We changed mules and continued our way, which ran along the sea-shore for about half an hour, then left it for good.

September 21.—We traveled the whole night in the same way as above-mentioned. The morning brought to our view a mountainous and unimproved country. It was as wild as the Rocky Mountains. The ravines were the only part of the country which was cultivated, and they were planted with Indian corn and chestnut-trees.

The houses of the villages are all of stone, but they have a most wretched and miserable appearance. Poverty, dirt, and laziness are every where to be seen. The fields are not cultivated with the same care as in Switzerland. Here and there you meet patches of turnips, some of which are hoed by women, but this must be considered so much work thrown away, as they generally are not hoed at all.

At eight o'clock we arrived in a village where we expected to have a good breakfast, and, after such a ride, by all means a good wash. To our great disappointment, we had neither the one nor the other. Water there was plenty in the well; and as for the good breakfast, it reduced itself down to a cup of chocolate and something which we were told was coffee. We did not choose to experiment, so we chose the chocolate, which was in a little cup, two inches in diameter and three deep. These measures were reckoned on the outside of the cup, not on the inside. For this they charged us the moderate sum of ten *reals*. It is such an unaccustomed thing, without doubt, to see persons wash in this country, that they thought if we could wash we could pay.

After this sumptuous breakfast we went on again, and about eleven o'clock we reached the valley. It is large, extensive rolling ground, having no trees and looking like a desert. There is some grain grown, which consists of oats, barley, and a little wheat, but no corn. The grain is all planted in rows, and hilled up, like corn out West, only on two sides, not all around. The planting is done by dropping the seed after the plow has raised up the ground. I could not ascertain what an acre yielded, for no one either in the stage or in the village could inform me.

At one o'clock we arrived at Vittoria, where we got a kind of dinner. We even had the luxury of getting one towel for eight of us. Happy was he who found a clean corner! Thirty minutes after, we were again on the way through this dreary, desert-looking country. It is uninteresting, altogether without trees, and has not even a sign of cultivation. There are no houses on the plains; the villages are small, dirty, and miserable-looking; the houses have no windows to them except some few; the means of transportation is by mules, donkeys, and miserable two-wheeled carts. The cart-wheels are made wholly of plank, and then an iron tire is put on. We saw neither carriages nor wagons, but we met now and then a large two-wheeled car, with eight to sixteen mules hitched on, one in front of the other, stretching out a long way.

On our left I saw men working on the railway which is eventually to go from Bayonne to Madrid. Even this enterprise is carried on by Frenchmen.

We sped on at the expense of the lungs and whip of the driver and conductor. Neither the one nor the other were spared. I thought that the whip bill would be very dear to the company, but I learned that the driver furnishes his own whip. We arrived in a dirty little town, where, to our great astonishment, we were told to get out to have our baggage again inspected. I tried to ascertain the reason for twice inspecting your baggage in the same country, but I was unsuccessful. "It must be done;" that was all I could learn. After inspecting us as well as our trunks, they permitted us to go on. We almost got ourselves in trouble before leaving this place; for, as we were going along its street at a sharp walk, up jumped a man of authority telling the driver to stop, and accusing him of trotting in the street. The conductor, driver, and postillion all protested against this false accusation. A dispute arose; high words ensued; and then the man of authority threatened to sue the conductor, driver, postillion, and even the passengers. Hearing this, and foreseeing the little chance of justice here, I suggested to the conductor to put an end to all lawsuits by driving on, and this time at full speed. He took the hint, and away we went, scattering all the men of authority right and left, none venturing to stop us. That was putting an end to a lawsuit pretty quick, and for once again we were out of trouble. The country through which we passed was just the same as I have already described above.

September 22.—We arrived at Burgos, at the railway station, at four o'clock in the morning. Here our whole diligence, baggage and all, except passengers, was hoisted upon a car, and fastened to it. We were furnished seats in the cars. I was very much astonished at seeing such a great number of people at the station, and especially so, because Burgos did not seem large enough to furnish so many travelers. There was an immense mass of men, women, and children, all crowding toward the ticket-office. When the doors were open, there was a general rush and scramble for seats. The enigma was soon explained to me. It was not Burgos alone that produced all this people, but the whole country around; they were all bound for Valladolid, where there was to be a bull-fight lasting four days.

We were unable to get the least thing to eat at Burgos. At the next station all the extra cars were put on, but they were hardly sufficient to hold all the people here, who were also on their way to the bull-fight.

The master of the train, conductor, and other officers ran right and left, swore, cursed, blasphemed, thus making the confusion tenfold greater and the delay much longer. The consequence of all this was that we only got off one hour and a half later than we should have done by the regulations. The train at last started, but, being more than the locomotive could easily draw, our progress was slow. At the next station hundreds were waiting to be taken in, but the master of the train only went slow enough to tell the chief of the station that there were no more places, as all was full. Though the cars were in motion, no sooner was this heard than there was a general pursuit, some succeeding in scrambling into the cars or gaining the top. This was followed by a general groaning and cursing from those who were unsuccessful, and loud cheers of hurrah from those who had succeeded in getting in or climbing on top of the cars.

I pitied the poor ticket officer. As I turned round my head in that direction I saw already a crowd forming round him, making most violent gesticulations—no doubt asking back their money, with damage and interest for bets which they never would have made. If physiognomy shows the workings of the human mind, that of the poor fellows who were left evinced the most bitter disappoinment. Napoleon witnessing the burning of Moscow could not have looked as deplorable as these poor people who were left.

We traveled six hours in the railway, after which we again got into the diligence, to which fourteen mules were put, and off we went. At ten o'clock P.M. we arrived at another railway station, where we learned that we were one hour too late. Our conductor swore at the manager, and the manager swore at the conductor, each blaming the other. At last they came to terms. It was mutually agreed that it would not happen again till next time;

and we were made to understand that a merchandise train would carry us to Madrid.

The passengers at first seemed to like the delay, for they had had nothing to eat for sixteen hours, and they thought it would be a fine opportunity to refill their empty stomachs. We all ran to the dépôt like so many famished wolves. But what was our disappointment when they informed us that the station was quite new, and that there was nothing eatable to be had. After a long hunt, we found, in a corner, a woman who sold *aguardiente* and some bad water.

Dear reader, you ought to have seen the faces of the Johnny Bulls, the Johnny Crapauds, your Yankee commissioner, and his starved secretary. The scale had turned; the chevaliers of the bull-fight would have burst into a laugh had they seen our ludicrous expressions. How we did "bless" the conductors and managers in general, and ours in particular! We walked up and down the yard in a rage, dining on the dust our feet kicked up, and having the beauty of the moon for dessert. At last the Spanish hour arrived which is marked two on my watch, and we were packed into the baggage train. Our diligence was along with us. The whistle blew, and we started.

Our train got in at the Madrid station at one o'clock in the morning. Here we again got into our diligence, and were wheeled to the office of the company in the city. The Custom-house officers detained us for a while, after which, to our great relief, we were allowed to go.

We went to the Hôtel des Ambassadeurs. Of course, every one was asleep. We managed, however, to get a room, and the waiter, seeing our forlorn looks, brought us a bottle of wine, and then, with great mystery, drew from his pocket two cakes, called *ladies' fingers*, from their size, no doubt, and, putting them beside the wine, told us that no charge would be made for them. Fatigued with our fifty-six hours' ride, we crawled into our beds, sure that we would not have the nightmare from an overcharged stomach.

September 23.—After ten o'clock A.M. we took a carriage and drove to the residence of the American minister, but found that he, his family, and secretary were at Lagrange, the summer residence of the queen. From here we drove round the city, visiting the palace, the gardens, the promenades, the Prado, etc. We also visited the fair, which was being held on the continuation of the Prado, on the edge of the city.

In this fair is offered for sale every thing which can be imagined used for household or domestic economy, from a spoon to
a stove, a canary-bird to a hare, a needle to a dress, a ring to a
diamond, a sheet of paper to a library, a knife to a plow; and, in
fact, every thing which is made use of in domestic economy, as
well as many that are not.　I found nothing worthy of note here,
and, in fact, I may say that Madrid fell far below my expecta-
tions.　There are many provincial cities in Europe which are
much handsomer.

The royal palace is large and very good-looking.　It is very
plain, having little ornament and no statues.　The statues round
the circular garden in front of the palace are none the better for
wear.　They are hewn out of some sandstone instead of marble,
and represent the ancient kings and queens of Spain, besides
some of its heroes.　The garden itself is pretty handsome.　The
palace is on a splendid elevation at one end of the city, but what
a dreary, barren waste is seen from it!　This waste commences
almost under the walls of the palace.　There is nothing to relieve
the eye; no green, no meadows, no woods, no gardens, no cha-
teaux—not even farms.　All that is seen is stubble-fields, and
now and then a brick-manufactory.　Even the queen's garden is
of little consequence, and looks most sadly neglected.　The streets
are not better, if even as good as those of San Francisco.　The
world-renowned Prado has miserable old stumpy trees, half decayed, ill kept, and possesses dust enough to frighten any man
who has black boots.

However, Madrid has one advantage over all Europe and America, and that is its fountain, which plays in the middle of the
square of the city.　It has no ornaments whatever, simply a basin,
which is 100 feet in diameter, in the centre of which is an iron
pipe about four inches in diameter.　This sends out a stream of
water which rises to 170 feet.　Seen from a distance, it looks like
snow curling up from the ground.　The Botanic Gardens are in
progress, and promise well.

But I have neglected to give an account of the country through
which we traveled.　It was a wide plain, cultivated with wheat,
barley, and oats.　The people live in villages; therefore from
one town to the other there is nothing to break the monotony of
the plain—no haystack, house, or even pile of rocks.　The villages in the plains consist of low and miserable houses.　In the
streets there are probably one or two shops, the whole value of
the place being $500, if so much.

We passed one village, which, with a few exceptions, was built in the ancient style of the renowned city of Petra, in Arabia; only, instead of being hewn in the rock, the houses, or rather cellars, are dug in a clay hill. Here in the cellars, without windows, the people live. In the rear of these habitations is a hole which serves for a chimney.

On the plains of New Mexico, famous for their numerous squirrels, their holes are called villages; but what shall I call this? my English is too defective to give it an appropriate name.

On approaching Valladolid, I saw some few vines planted, but without stakes, and allowed to grow as they pleased, having about five to eight feet distance between. They are plowed by a yoke of oxen; afterward the ground is piled up around them. Corn and potatoes are also planted. The soil is sandy and yellow; and the wine I tasted was most rascally stuff, being made worse by being kept in hide bags made of calves' skin. Vines continue to be planted in spots almost all the way to Madrid.

At eight o'clock in the evening we started from Madrid, on our way toward Malaga. We were drawn to the railroad dépôt by six fine gray horses. Here we all got out, and, to my great astonishment, the hundred buckles holding up the baggage were undone, and all taken off and put into the cars. The distance from the diligence office to the railway station was only from ten to fifteen minutes' ride, and I could not make out why all that trouble was taken to put on our baggage, when it had to be taken off again so soon. Why not give the passengers a rendezvous at the station? Much time and trouble would be saved them. To all my inquiries no one could give an answer. They have few practical ideas here at present. When all the baggage was removed the diligence was taken back to the city, where the horses will remain a day and a half idle.

After some whistling, backing, etc., we started, and soon lost sight of Madrid. The moon was beautiful, and, as I lay in my seat looking out of the window, I imagined myself back in New Mexico traveling in cars. There was, in fact, some resemblance, except that on the Plains we sometimes pass a cottonwood-tree; here not a bush could be seen. Passing several villages, all 'desolate and uninviting, we at last came to the place where we had again to take the diligence. It was two in the morning. When the baggage came into the baggage-room there was a general rush, each passenger laying his hands upon any thing that came within reach, whether his own or not. When his hands were full, he hunted for the person who had his own, and then reclaimed it, making a mutual exchange. The scene was highly comical, and worthy the pencil of Cruikshank, or Cham, or M'Lenan. When all had reclaimed their effects, there was found to be one package unreclaimed. Here a long parley ensued between the conductor and the railroad officers. They counted and recounted all the luggage, but to no effect. The passengers were all called up, to see if any one would claim the package. I was very much amused at the occurrence, as I felt satisfied that mine was all right, having watched it during every change from Madrid to this place. When the little struggle took place for the baggage, I heroically withstood several fierce attacks on my little valise and carpet bag. Not being able to find an owner for the package, it was laid down, and there took place—a stand-still.

We walked up and down an hour waiting for something to turn up. All this time the mules were hitched to the diligence upon which was the luggage; but, to our astonishment, no order was given us to mount. At last the cold atmosphere had its effect upon the brains of the passengers, who became uneasy, and they began questioning each other as to the reason for not starting. As no one could answer, impatience soon turned to anger, and one person stepped up to the conductor, who was musingly leaning against a pillar, and asked him for an explanation. He answered that it was on account of this package, for which he was responsible; he was certain it belonged to some one in the diligence, and he could not take it out of the dépôt until some one claimed it; then, again, if he left it behind, the company were responsible for it to the owner, and he did not wish to get himself into trouble. His answer was cool and philosophical. It was in vain the passengers grew angry; his calmness did not desert him.

So matters stood when the passengers gathered together again, and consulted vehemently on the subject. At last, when their indignation was fully aroused, they determined to go to a fellow-passenger who was a *Delegado,* and rouse his energy to action. This important person was calmly seated on a sofa, wrapped up in a warm cloak, thinking of his greatness, or, perhaps, whether Mexico should or should not be again annexed to Spain. In his dream of great things he had altogether forgotten little ones, and had not even noticed our delay—thanks to his comfortable coat. The passengers delegated him to represent them to the conductor. The *Delegado* was so much taken by the gravity and importance of the position, that he walked up to the conductor and demanded an immediate start. The demand was followed by the desired effect. A consultation was opened, and thus concluded: "Since every passenger present apparently had his baggage, and since every passenger in the diligence denied being the possessor of the package in question, it was decided that the named package did not belong to any of the passengers; therefore, if left, the company would not be responsible for it."

This decision was received with applause, and soon we were galloping away. This delay, caused by these disputes, occupied two and a half hours. Of course, myself and son, being the only foreigners in the diligence, kept quiet. One reason for our not interfering was the fact that we were Americans, who are held in great dislike in this country. Even the deputy's face beamed with smiles when we at last started.

We had made but a few hundred yards when we were stopped and counted head by head. Yankee-like, I stuck my head out of the window to see what now was in the wind. I saw the conductor, driver, postillion, and an aid gathered around the door of a house, disputing violently. In the door were two men—one a gendarme, with his carbine; the other with a paper in his hand. The latter said, firmly, that we could not be allowed to proceed, as we had one more person in the diligence than the law allows. All wanted to speak at a time, so that a confusion ensued in which none understood what the other said. Finally, the conductor succeeded in "getting the floor" alone. He remonstrated, saying that the person who was too much was a young child sitting on his mother's lap, and could not be separated from her; besides this, as she had her husband, it would be cruel to separate them from one another. Notwithstanding this eloquent appeal to humanity, the man with the paper remained inflexible. Nothing could move him, until one passenger, far away from the boy, declared that the child was very small, did not occupy any place, since he was on his mother's lap, and that he was not at all troublesome. At this declaration, and its unanimity (namely, one man), the official yielded, and we went on.

However, doubts soon arose in my mind whether the person who so generously pleaded the cause of the boy had not better change seats with me, at least for a time. The little fellow went to sleep leaning his head and whole body on me. Now, as the road was not over smooth, the diligence sometimes gave a jerk on one side, sometimes on the other, and the child followed its movements. Imagine what a pleasant position I was in. I would much rather have been on a "grizzly" hunt. Three nights previous I had not slept. However, I consoled myself with the idea that all my pains would be remunerated by a sweet smile from the daughter of "a hundred dons of old renown" when daylight came. I awaited daylight with impatience. At last it came, and I found the *señora* of my dreams not very ugly, not very old, but very dirty.

Near seven o'clock the conductor announced to us that we were to breakfast in the village which we were then entering. No sooner had our feet touched the ground than we were surrounded by about thirty beggars. They really besieged us. Resistance was out of the question. In the first place, it would not look well to attack a lot of old men and women, all blind, lame, or diseased; then they were in greater number than we. I was struck by an idea: putting my hand in my pockets, I pulled out a handful of copper coin and threw it among the crowd. The move was most successful; there was a general scramble, in which the lame walked and the blind saw. While they were still scrambling for the money, we gained the inn by the road which they had left open to us. Once in the tavern, we were safe, unless we approached the door, when they began making a piteous noise, begging in the most moving language. This invariably happened whenever we approached the door, and we as invariably made a hasty and disorderly retreat to the interior.

A couple of miles on the other side of Balde Pengas the vine plantations begin again. The soil is either of sand or clay, or a mixture of the two. The wine is fermented in large clay jars from six to eight, or even ten feet high. The wine has a peculiar and disagreeable taste, which makes it almost impossible to drink it after it has once come in contact with the palate. This comes from the hides which the wine is put in. They have no barrels. Every ordinary wine that I have yet drank in Spain has in it either aguardiente or alcohol; this renders them unfit for common use, for they naturally are very strong already.

The fifteen minutes allowed for breakfast over, we huddled in again to our places. The little boy, being tired of sitting on his mother's lap, took half of his mother's seat and half of mine, which was already not too large before. However, I managed to squeeze myself some way. The heat was intense, and the dust intolerable, for it was as fine as it was penetrating. Away we went, followed by four or five little girls and boys, who ran alongside of the diligence begging. The girls gave up in about three fourths of a mile; the boys held out longer, and one of them ran for at least four miles. We had thrown out to them some coppers from time to time. Neither the girls nor boys wore shoes.

Our way led us near to the railway which was being built; we saw hundreds of men and women working on it. They all of them had on their backs a basket hardly holding four to five gallons; they would creep snail-like to where the dirt was found, fifteen to twenty yards off, leisurely fill the basket, and then return in a manner so slow that the slowest man in America would become desperate. When they arrived at the place where the load was to be deposited, they threw it down, but always in the most careful manner. These railway contractors seem not to have the least practical idea; had they one, they would have all this transportation done by machinery. We passed several other places where they were also working, but all in the same snail-like way.

The mountains are all barren; not a tree can be seen. Now and then we passed a miserable village filled with beggars. You can not walk, stand, or sit any where without being besieged by them. It is the most annoying thing that can be imagined; they will not be contented with a simple refusal, but will obstinately follow you up wherever you go.

We at last reached the top of the mountain, where we found a table-land. It was here that we saw the ancient Moorish town of Carolina. It is a thriving village, and surrounded, as far as the eye can reach, by olive-trees; these furnish a most pleasing contrast with the barren country through which we had passed since we left Bayonne.

We were several hours passing through this really beautiful country, when we arrived at the place where we were to dine. Victoria, I believe, was the name of the place. I succeeded, in spite of their numbers, in making my way through the beggars, and coming to the kitchen. I seized upon the first thing which fell under my hands and looked like a wash-bowl. After washing my face, I was lucky enough to find a clean corner to wipe it. Our dinner was a Spanish one. What was wanting in dishes

was made up in charges. The conductor did not leave us much
time to dispute the charges, but hustled us into the diligence, and
away we went. Our road still led us through many beautiful
olive and vine plantations. The boy settled the right to the seat
by taking up the largest half of it. Night soon set in and veiled
the scenery from our view. As darkness came on, the boy returned to his mother's lap, to my great relief, for when he went
to sleep I only had to support half of him. Arrived at Jean, several passengers left us, and the lady with her little boy went into
the Rotonde. Her place was taken by a gentleman, and from
here we enjoyed a little more comfort.

We entered Granada at ten o'clock in the morning. It is an
old Moorish town, has quite a considerable population, and, from
what I could see, was quite thriving. Its produce is olives, oil,
wine, hemp, and lead. This latter article is found in quite large
quantities in the neighborhood. The hotels are miserable, and
their prices exorbitant, as myself and fellow-passengers can all
testify.

September 24.—We were informed that the stage would only
leave at seven in the evening, so we would have time to see every thing. I went to a hotel, engaged a guide, and ordered him
to get me saddle-horses to see the celebrated Alhambra. He soon
returned, informing me that he could not get saddle-horses, but
that he had engaged a carriage for three dollars. Informing me
that the stable where the carriage was lay on the way to the Alhambra, I thought that we might walk to it. He advised me to
do so, saying that it would save time. This phrase "save time"
sounded pleasantly in my ear, for it was so long since I had last
heard it. It did not astonish me, for our guide, who was a young
Spaniard, had lived some time in America.

What was our astonishment and indignation on seeing our carriage, which was no more or less than a very old two-wheeled
Spanish cart, without springs. It had two boards on the inside
for seats, with rags for cushions, held up on the sides by ropes.
After some grumbling we got in. The concern was drawn by a
large bony mule, led by the driver, who walked alongside, and
occasionally gave him a poke in the ribs with the butt of his
whip, which had a nail in its end. As we rode in the streets we
looked out to see if any one was looking at us, but no one paid
any attention to our "carriage," so we came to the conclusion
that it was the customary mode of traveling here.

We continued our way slowly through the narrow, winding streets until we came to the garden gates. In due time we arrived at the Generalife. It was here that we perceived how finely our guide had taken us in. In the first place, the walk through the streets would have been much more agreeable than the horrible shaking and jolting of our cart; secondly, the distance was very short; and, lastly, the walk would have been a most agreeable one through all the beautiful and shady alleys.

I will not attempt a description of this beautiful palace, which is considered the finest the world ever had. For that I refer my readers to Washington Irving. Only he has done justice to the beautiful palace, magnificent view, gardens, and legends. Read his "Legends of the Alhambra," and you will be here.

When I had sufficiently admired the scenery and all the beauties of the palace, I started down on foot, not caring to rub off the small part of skin still remaining on my shins. My son, however, thought to make the most of a bad thing, and so went in the carriage to the Cartuja, celebrated for its interior architectural beauty, and the mad-house, which was an ancient convent, built by Ferdinand and Isabella, in accordance with a vow which they had made to that effect while reducing Granada.

I inspected several manufactories, but none of them had any thing worth mentioning to my readers. I returned home and wrote up my journal.

I found much difficulty in reaching home on account of the beggars, who were not only in great numbers, but also very impertinent. They would cry out, "For God's sake, look at me, sir; I am old, sick, and in want." In looking at them I was often astonished how they could use such terms when they looked so well, and were neither old nor badly dressed. It seems to have passed into a habit with Spanish people. I really think that one third are beggars. Some Spanish gentlemen informed me that it was not considered as derogating from one's dignity to beg.

We left Granada in full speed at seven o'clock, and almost ran down a dozen soldiers who were drilling. They were marching in double file toward the road. The conductor thought that they would halt, and the captain thought that the diligence would stop, and so both continued, until the men, seeing their danger, broke the ranks and fell back, no doubt thinking that they would be safer farther off than under the wheels. What the captain thought I don't know. The conductor did not stop to ask his opinion on the subject.

Our seats were pretty comfortable, they having placed us into the Berline, as they call it here. We tried in Madrid to get the same seats which we had in coming from Bayonne, but they had already been taken.

I could not judge of the appearance of the country, as it was dark and cloudy. When daybreak came we were on high mountains, planted from the valleys to their very tops with grape-vines. The soil is red and rocky. The appearance of the country was very picturesque, as on the tops of the mountains, on their sides and in the ravines, houses were built. This was the first time I witnessed in Spain an idea of practical life. This is certainly far better than huddling themselves together in dirty little villages. Not only is it more healthy, more comfortable, but it is also more profitable.

The mountains are very steep, so the cultivation must be done by hoes; the work, however, is not overdone. It does not rain for seven or eight months during the year, consequently but little grass grows. Even if it did rain, the weeds would not come up very fast in such poor ground.

The wine of the mountains has the taste and look of dark sherry, and, if care was taken in making it, it would become an excellent wine. The people here seem to make no improvement whatever; their wine is still made in the same manner that the Romans employed when masters of the country.

Our road still wound up the hill for some time, and vineyards were planted from the foot to the top of the mountains. Arriving at last on the top of the mountain, we had a magnificent view of Malaga and its fertile valley. The prospect was beautiful, and for a moment I forgot all my road troubles in looking on the scene which lay before me. All was smiling to me; the large plantations of olive-trees, vines, oranges, and lemons; Malaga with its manufactories; the old Moorish citadel and its cathedral—all present a most pleasing view, which called out admiration when from the town you turned your eyes toward the sea, sprinkled here and there with white sails. My pleasure in beholding this scene was not a little enhanced by the thought that at last my traveling by diligence would end.

Descending the mountain, we passed several raisin-making establishments. They are very numerous around Malaga.

We soon reached the city, and proceeded to the Alameda Hotel, which proved to be an excellent one. After having well washed ourselves and breakfasted, we were but too glad to lie down and take a sleep of several hours. We needed it after the six or seven days or nights that we had passed in the diligence.

When our dinner was taken we went to the Alameda, or promenade, where there was to be music. Here we saw all the fashionable people promenading up and down, among whom were many dark-eyed señoritas. After listening for some time to the music, which was very good, I returned to the hotel to write, and my son Arpad went to the theatre.

September 27.—In the morning we hired three horses, two for ourselves and one for our guide. Our steeds proved to be fine ones of the Andalusian race. We first proceeded to the dwelling of a nurseryman, but, not finding him at home, we went to the vine plantation of Don Luis Arra de Breka. This vineyard is 200 *fanegas* in extent. It makes 5000 boxes of raisins, 15,000 *arobas* of Malaga wine, and 300 *arobas* of vinegar. A box of raisins weighs twenty-five American pounds, and a barrel one hundred pounds. An aroba contains twenty-two bottles of wine, and a fanega of land contains fifteen hundred vines. These statistics were furnished by the overseer, who readily gave us all the information we desired. The establishment employs sixty men in selecting, drying, and packing the raisins.

The drying-grounds consist of an elevation whose surface makes an inclination of forty-five degrees, whose length is sixty feet, and width twelve. It is built out of brick when a natural elevation can not be found. The drying-grounds are separated from each other by bricks stuck into the ground. These bricks are about eighteen inches long, one and a half inches thick, and six wide. The floor is a clay soil, overspread naturally or artificially with small loose pebbles. It resembles somewhat a threshing-floor, only is not so hard. The grapes, when ripe, are brought and placed on these drying-grounds, which are invariably built facing the noon sun, that they may receive the greatest possible heat. It is to obtain this effect that these grounds are inclined forty-five degrees, for it is at this inclination that the heat is the greatest.

The grapes, laid simply on the ground as above mentioned, will naturally become dusty, or have some particles of dust; therefore I asked why they did not spread them on a canvas or on straw mats. The answer I received was, that neither canvas nor straw received as much heat as the ground, and, consequently, the latter would dry the grapes much quicker than the former. With all this, I believe that many improvements might be made in their manner of making raisins. Asphaltum, well mixed with sand, being black, would receive a very great amount of heat from the sun.

The drying-grounds are every evening covered over with boards, one overlaying the other, so that no rain or dew may reach the grapes during the process of drying. The grapes are left on the grounds eight, ten, and twelve days, according to the weather and their progress in curing. But, inasmuch as the size and ripeness of the grape comes in for a large part, they do not dry all at once; and so, when the attendant sees some which are ready, three or four men are put to work at the lower ends, to pick out those which are cured, gradually proceeding upward. They are seated on a plank resting on the separating bricks, and have on their laps small boxes which hold about eight pounds of raisins. These raisins are afterward taken into the adjoining pack-house, where a person with a pair of scissors cuts out all the rotten or inferior grapes. It is then passed to the *Selector*, who selects all the fine large grapes, and puts them in a box beside him, of the same dimensions as the former. The other raisins are left in their own box, and filled up afterward from the second quality of succeeding boxes. The first class is passed, when the box is full, to the weigher, who fills up what is wanting, and takes out what is too much; each must hold exactly six and a quarter pounds of raisins. It then goes to the *packer*, who upsets the raisins into a box of the same dimensions lined with paper; afterward he puts them in a transporting box, which contains four such small ones, and weighs twenty-five pounds. Each six and a quarter pounds is separated from the other by the above-named paper. If the paper is taken by the corners, the raisins may be taken out six and a quarter pounds by six and a quarter pounds without disturbing them or their order. In fine large raisins these four layers of paper are absolutely necessary to each twenty-five pounds, as they absorb the must of the grapes, which, to preserve their size, have not been completely dried, as that would shrink them up considerably. The second quality is treated in the same manner in every respect as the first. The only difference between them is their size.

The berries which were cut out by the scissors are all thrown into a barrel, and then taken to the press-house; there they are trodden by men with shoes; then the pressed juice runs from the press into a large vat-like hole, made out of bricks and plastered with Roman cement. It is dipped out from here with buckets like water from a well, the juice being almost as thick as tar. Then it is taken to large vats or barrels. In large establishments the barrels or vats are made of oak, but in smaller establishments there are large earthen jars holding from ten to two hundred and fifty gallons.

When the juice is poured into these jars or tanks, to each ten gallons of juice one gallon of aguardiente or brandy is put. It is then left to ferment slowly, no more care being taken of it for six months, when it is drawn into a new barrel. As is well known, the Malaga wine requires six to eight years to make it good and marketable. It is very heavy, and extremely sweet. Not much is used by Americans; England and Russia consume the most of it.

The residue—skins, stems, seeds, etc.—after being thoroughly pressed, is put into a large cemented vat; a large quantity of water is thrown on, washing it thoroughly. This artificial juice is let run down into a well made of bricks and cement, where it is left to form itself into vinegar, and, when ready, it is drawn off and sent to market.

Besides the above-described drying-plots of forty-five degrees, there are here also twenty to thirty drying-plots which are almost level. The floor is similar to the ones described. The width is, however, twenty-five feet, and, instead of being covered in the night or rainy days with boards, a canvas is used, so arranged that it can be brought on or off the ground by drawing a cover across a pole. This seems to be the better method, as much labor is required to lift the boards, which must be done by two men, and piece by piece.

There are two drying-places in the vineyard and two packing-houses, to one of which is attached the wine-house and press. There are no cellars, the wine being kept in a large room in a stone house.

In the same place are raised and dried fifteen to twenty thousand pounds of figs, which are dried in the same manner and upon plots as the grapes; only instead of being lightly pressed into the bags and boxes, they are solidly pressed; for the more they are pressed, the more saccharine they become. Figs require ten to fifteen days in curing. The pressure must be just heavy enough to flatten the figs without smashing them. The fig-trees are planted promiscuously, whereas the almond-trees, of which many are raised, are planted in avenues.

The vines are planted two *varras* apart. They are kept low to the ground, and are trimmed to one size. According to the thickness and strength of the vine, it has four to eight shoots. The vine is pruned every year to one eye, and forms a kind of knob or head. The shoots are not staked, but left to run on the ground. After the month of June the ground is gathered up around the vine as we hill potatoes. This is done to permit the sun to fall on the roots and draw the heat to the grapes. The vines are thrifty, and the soil is red and gravelly.

We arrived at a packing-house; the servant took our horses and tied them separately. As I was taking notes I heard a terrible stampede. Running out to see the cause, I found that one of the horses had pulled off the bridle and "pitched into" the one standing next him. The third one, also wishing to have a hand in the matter, broke his bridle, and the fight went on lustily. The third, being somewhat inferior, soon gave up, after receiving several kicks and bites, but the others fought like tigers. We tried to stop the fight, but no whip, stone, or pole could separate the combatants. A score or more of men surrounded them, but in vain. One of the men threw a stone at one of the horses, but it missed its mark, and landed in the stomach of my son, almost knocking him down. At last they were separated; but what a sight! They were bleeding every where, and the bridles and saddles were all in pieces. I contemplated the scene before me, and the figure of my landlord rose up before my vision like the ghost in Hamlet. I saw in imagination a long paper with a fearful column of figures, the sum total at the bottom being quite too long to be read.

After patching up our bridles and saddles, we remounted for the city. I was hungry, having started without breakfast, but my appetite was considerably decreased by the vision of the coming bill. At last we arrived, and rode to the stable. I watched my man. He looked at his horses, shook his head, told me he must send for a veterinary surgeon, etc. This calmness foreboded no good. It showed diplomacy, which I determined to meet with the same. I went to our consul, Mr. Hancock, an excellent gentleman, by the way. I told him my suspicions about breakers ahead. The consul immediately sent his clerk to the Civil Register's office to have our names registered; this would make the matter more complicated for the stable-man to get an exorbitant judgment for damages. So the matter rests; and so I must retire without knowing how far my pocket will be drained.

September 28.—At seven we started again with the same Andalusian steeds, who were oiled, and the bridles patched up. The owner and I exchanged no words. After riding five miles we arrived at the residence of General Concha, the military governor of Granada. On this property there are many olive-trees, also an olive-mill, which is very simple, consisting of a round stone basin with a conic stone in the middle, which is pulled by a horse or mule. The stone crushes the olives; the olives are then put into a screw-press. By this means the oil is extracted and runs into the stone basin, and from there through a trough into a barrel. The Spaniards do not refine their oil like the French or Italians, and it sells for less, though it is really finer. It is used with all the sediment. This makes it disagreeable in cooked dishes. Sixty olive-trees are planted on one fanega of land; grain or vines are raised between. The olive-trees, being planted near to the sea, do not do so well as in the district of Cordova, where the average production is twenty-five pounds of oil to the tree. Here not more than half as much is yielded. One aroba of oil is sold for fifty-eight to sixty reals—about three dollars.

On our road we passed a cotton manufactory, where cloth is made by a New Orleans company. We saw an iron or smelting establishment, also owned by foreigners, but of what nation I did not learn. To the right and left of the road there is a great deal of sugar-cane, which is ground by a mill in Malaga.

After examining the trees and the olive gathering, which is now beginning, we returned to the city, having engaged from a nursery-man in the office and presence of our consul several thousand of raisin-vines, olive, pomegranate, pepper, orange, fig, lemon, and other trees. I visited several prominent merchants, to whom I was introduced by Mr. Hancock.

As I was leaving my hotel I saw a herd of goats. Their owner was hallooing "*Leche! Leche!*" loud enough to wake the dead. As he was screaming, people ran from the houses with pails. These he took, set down by the goats, and milked the pail full, received his money, and satisfied his customers. This is a certain way of getting unadulterated milk. This was not entirely new to me, as I saw it tried by a Frenchman with cows in San Fran-

cisco, but he gave up the business on account of having no customers.

After a good dinner with the consul we made our arrangements for departure to-morrow by the steamer for Alicante. I
found that no steamer goes to Portugal, as they would have to
stay in quarantine, as the yellow fever has broken out in the south
of France. I was disappointed, as I intended to visit Oporto;
but then the vine disease is universal, and I may have introduced
it into our state.

September 29.—After paying our bills, which were very high,
we started for the steamer. Mr. Hancock accompanied us, but
before sent his clerk, Don Luis, to the police-office and French
consul, to have our passports go through all the annoying formal-
ities; but, as Don Luis had no breakfast, and not finding the consul at home, he gave the passports to the porter. He returned
in a short time, and found that the porter had taken a trip in the
country, taking the passports with him. This annoyed Don Luis;
but, like a prudent general, he made out two others, had them
viséd, and came down just in time for the consul to sign them.
Mr. Hancock "blew up" Don Luis for leaving the passports, bade
us adieu, and we jumped into the boat just in time. The many
attentions I have received from Mr. Hancock will ever keep him
in my remembrance.

I may here mention that all the harbors in the south, as Genoa,
Marseilles, Malaga, etc., have no wharf, but you are obliged to
embark in small boats. This makes it very inconvenient, particularly for ladies. The shipping is very close together, and in
passing along one is often inundated with slop-water. It is really
astonishing how little progress these people are making. We
started at twelve o'clock precisely in an iron steamer, the *Paris*.
We kept close to the shore, passing the fertile valley of Malaga,
and sailed by her high mountains, all covered with vines and vil-
las. Soon, however, steep, rocky, barren mountains took the place
of the beautiful fertile valleys. Night set in, and with it a furi-
ous wind, which kept increasing so much that nearly all the passengers were sea-sick, and the steamer was delayed full ten hours,
arriving at Alicante at eleven o'clock at night.

October 1.—The steamer remaining two days, it gave me an
opportunity of examining the neighborhood, and engaging such
vines and trees as the country possesses. First I went to the
market, where I found some grapes which I do not yet possess.

From there I presented myself to the American consul, Mr. Leach, and made arrangements with him to send to Havre the vines I had purchased. After visiting the neighborhood, which is not very inviting, we returned to the steamer, which lay anchored in the harbor.

October 2.—This morning was fine and clear. At nine o'clock the cargo arrived, and was speedily hoisted into the steamer, which then left. We passed several valleys planted with olives, figs, vines, etc. They all looked very well, but the valleys are few, and there are numerous high, barren, rocky mountains.

October 3.—This morning opened calm and pleasant, but we were out of sight of land. As we neared shore, we met thousands of fishing-boats, with "shoulder of mutton" sails. The fishing trade is extensively carried on at Barcelona, Alicante, and other villages on this coast. The fish are caught in large quantities, and packed in olive oil. The coast is well populated. Numerous villages are scattered over the hills and valleys. Figs and olives are the principal produce. This part of Spain—Catalonia—is the richest in produce and manufactures; the people are more industrious.

We arrived at Barcelona at twelve o'clock. The steamer remaining four hours, we took a small boat and landed. The city is a busy commercial town. The shops are fine; the goods come from all countries; but the streets are narrow, as in all towns of Southern Europe. It has several fine public buildings, monuments, promenades, and squares. The population was stated to me at 160,000, but I doubt the number. There are large and numerous manufactories here of cotton, iron cutlery, woolen, etc. The harbor is full of vessels; the wharf full of grain, peas, corn, oats, fruit of all descriptions. The grain is put loose in the ship-holds, and when it is to be moved it is put into bags, taken ashore, emptied into a pile, then again put in bags to be taken away. This is a very awkward way of doing business, particularly as there are linen manufactories, and linen is cheap. The sardine fishery is in full operation now, and the packing requires a great number of men.

I made some inquiry as to the making of the wine, which is not agreeable to drink; but a great deal is taken to Brazil, England, and even North America. Many varieties of grapes are mixed together, crushed with the feet, put into a vat; a good portion of lime is added, with which it ferments. The lime gives it a dark-

er color. The whole is fermented in a vat built of stone and cemented. The fermentation lasts from two to four days; is very
strong, as the lime aids it. When the fermentation stops, the
whole is drawn off and put into barrels, and often leather bags
made of hogs' or calves' skins. At the same time, one third or
one quarter of alcohol is added. The wine is used the same year,
but when alcohol is plenty it will keep for any length of time.
The same process is used in all the vineyards.

At five o'clock we left for Marseilles. The weather was fine.
We arrived October 4th. At ten o'clock we took the train for
Paris. Being night, I could see nothing. In the morning, however, we stopped at Lyons, the great silk manufactory of France.
The adjoining country is well cultivated. The people were busy
sowing wheat. The grain-lands extend to Villafranca, then vines
begin to predominate. Around Macon are planted all vines.

Tours and Chalons have partly vine and partly grain planted.
From Chalons to Dijon the whole country is planted with vines.
But I have already given a description of this country.

October 5.—Having arrived in Paris, I found letters awaiting me
there which demanded my immediate return home. Having visited all the prominent wine-growing countries except Hungary,
my return was at once resolved upon. It is true that my original intention was to visit Greece and Egypt; but, finding that
the plague had broken out in Syria, and I would have to remain
in quarantine for forty days, even if I escaped the sickness, I,
of course, decided not to go. Even if I had gone, I could have
thus done no service to the State, as the wine-making is still carried on in those countries according to the old plan. The vines
and cuttings I procured through the American consuls.

My determination to speed home was farther strengthened by
the fact that the Legislature would meet in the beginning of January, and would very likely be in session but a short time; and,
as I was required by the joint resolution to report before this
body, my preparations were soon made.

October 14.—I went to Havre to make the necessary arrangements there to receive the vines from all parts as already stated.
The vines were all to be directed to the American consul. Having made the arrangement with the consul and Messrs. William
Isilin & Co., we returned to Paris the next day, packed up our
traps, bade good-by to our new acquaintances, parted with our
family, whom we left behind partly because a stormy passage was

expected, and partly on account of my son, who is studying practically the manufacture of Champagne in Europe, and has been so engaged for the last year and a half, and whose apprenticeship will be out in the spring.

On our arrival we gave our attention to the drainage of lands. Went to London, thence to Liverpool. There we embarked on the English steamer Europa. After a stormy voyage of fifteen days, arrived in Boston; from thence to New York, and finally arrived in California December 5th.

CHAPTER IX.

GRAPES AND WINES IN CALIFORNIA.

The Author's Experience.—Climate.—Site.—Soil.—Plowing.—Laying out a Vineyard.—Digging Holes.—Planting.—Cultivating.—Pruning in different Years.—Summer Pruning.—Crushing.—Cost of Planting a Vineyard.—The Author's Expenditure on One hundred Acres.—Quality of the Author's Wines.—Mr. Szemere's Pamphlet.—Adulteration of Wine in Europe.—Quantity of Wine produced in France.—The Wines of Hungary.—Prospects of Wine Culture in California.—Statistics of Wine Culture in Europe. — Good and bad Years in Europe. — The Advantages of California as a Wine Country.

HAVING given the mode of planting and treating vineyards in different parts of Europe, we deem it necessary to say something of the mode of planting and treating vineyards in California.

It will be apparent to practical men, who have cultivated vines in this country, that for us to practice many of the systems in use in Europe would be unprofitable, either on account of the difference in climate, or the high price of labor in California. On this head, however, we do not anticipate any difficulty to our intelligent and reflecting planters, for they will soon determine which mode of cultivation is best adapted to our soil, climate, and price of labor. But, for a guide to beginners, we will give a few extracts from an essay written by the author for the State Agricultural Society in 1858. It should be remarked, however, that a farther experience of four years proves that some of the instructions laid down in this essay require modification. We have arrived at this conclusion by careful observation of our own, having a vineyard of some four hundred acres, which, to the best of our belief, is the largest in the United States. We frankly confess that the result of careful experiments, made on similar soils, has changed some of our opinions, and our error was clearly proved by observations on our late European tour. We hold that confessing an opinion formed to have been erroneous is not only proper, but a duty we owe to science.

Whenever, in the extract from the essay, a difference of opinion between what we then held and what we have since formed occurs, we will note it, giving our present experience on the subject.

Climate.—The California climate, with the exception of the sea-coast, especially where the prevailing western winds drive the fogs over the locality, is eminently adapted for the culture of grape-vines, and it is proved conclusively that no European locality can equal within two hundred per cent. its productiveness. The oldest inhabitants have no recollection of a failure in the crops of grapes. The production is fabulous; and there is no doubt in my mind that before long there will be localities discovered which will furnish as noble wines as Hungary, Spain, France, or Germany ever have produced. Vineyards planted in various counties, beginning at San Diego up to Shasta, have given magnificent results, and leave no doubt in the mind that the north is as favorable and productive as the south.

Site.—In California site is not so material as in European countries, especially where, during the summer season, a good deal of rain falls; and if the vineyard is not exposed during the whole day to the sun, the rain will rot and damage the grapes. California, having an even temperature, is warm and without rains in summer. Almost any locality will do; but if a western gentle slope can be obtained, by all means it should be taken.

Soil.—When the planter resolves to plant a vineyard, he should determine whether he is planting to produce grapes for wine or for market. If for the former, he must look for a soil which is made by volcanic eruptions, containing red clay and soft rocks, which will decay by exposure to the air. The more magnesia, lime, or chalk the soil contains, so much the better. This kind of soil never cracks, and retains the moisture during the summer admirably. Such a soil will produce a wine that will keep good for fifty or one hundred years, and improve annually; is not liable to get sour, or, when exposed to the air after one year old, to get turbid, and change color in the bottle or glass.

If such soil can not be found on the ground desired to be laid out for a vineyard, the second best may be taken, which is a shell-mound. There are many localities in this State, even as high as the mountain tops, where acres of land consist of decayed shells. Such soil will give a good wine in great abundance. The next best to the above soil is a gravelly clay, slightly mixed with sand, so that it will not crack. If it can be, red color or dark black;

but avoid gray clay, which bakes in summer. The last of all which may be used for the production of wine is a light sandy, gravelly soil. This will give an abundance of wine, but it will not keep for any length of time. It will soon change color and become sour when exposed to the air; and the only mode of keeping this kind of wine for years is by adding to it brandy or alcohol, which, of course, deprives it of its purity, and makes it injurious to the health of the consumer.

The soils described above are recommended for producing wine, as just stated; but for producing marketable table grapes, the planter should select a piece of ground which is a rich black gravelly or sandy loam, exceedingly mellow, as most of the alluvials are; and if well-rotten manure from sheep or cattle corrals can be obtained, it will pay well to haul it on the ground. To be prepared for the grape-vines, it should be moderately moist, though not too moist. In this State deserted Indian villages are often found. In such localities the soil is exceedingly rich. A bucketful of it in the hole of a vine will astonish the planter by its effect. Such soil as just now described, either made by nature or artificially, will produce magnificent bunches of grapes, with large berries, in an immense quantity, which, of course, will please the eye and palate, as the bulb or skin is thin, and consequently the best qualified for table use.

Plowing.—The best mode to plow the land is with the so-called "deep-tiller;" for with it, by putting three horses abreast, you can plow twelve inches deep, except the soil should be very rocky. Follow this plow, in the same furrow, with a common shovel-plow, or, as it is called in some places, bull-tongue. This simple instrument, with two horses attached to it, will tear up and pulverize the earth ten or twelve inches more in depth. There are various designs of subsoil plows, but most of them require a great moving power, and will not answer after all. The above-named "bull-tongue" is successfully used by many planters in Sonoma and Nape Valleys. But it matters very little what plows or subsoilers the planter uses, as long as he plows and subsoils his land from twenty to twenty-four inches.

Laying out the Vineyard.—It is sufficiently proved, by close observations in Europe and California, that the vine planted eight feet apart is the best mode, especially in California, where land is yet cheap and labor high. Vines planted at this distance can be worked with the shovel-plow and one horse. Eight feet is as close as persons ought to plant. If planted closer, the vines, when five or six years old, will branch out considerably, and in the months of May, June, and July, all the tender vines would be broken by using a horse and shovel-plow. The planter would be therefore compelled to employ hands with hoes, and this would cost, in the first instance, ten times as much as horse-power; and, secondly, it would not do as good work, for no man will hoe as deep as a shovel-plow goes. Persons laying out vineyards must not be miserly, but leave wide roads—say twelve feet; at least one road every fifteen rows, which would be one hundred and twenty feet apart. Otherwise, when the vines bear and the grapes are picked, the person picking them must carry a heavy basket a long distance, to the road where the cart stands to haul it to the press-house. In reality, no person will lose any thing in the crops on account of the road, for the rows adjoining each side of the road will bear more, as they have an additional four feet of ground to feed on. No planter should, under any circumstances, plant trees of any description in a vineyard. A vineyard must be a vineyard, and nothing else. I need not waste room here to direct how to lay out the rows. Every man knows that, and has his own mode for it; but a straight row in every direction is essential to a prosperous cultivation.

Digging Holes.—When the land is laid out as above recommended, and a stick staked at every point where a vine is to be planted, a hole must be dug twenty inches square, and about two feet deep. The ground from the hole is to be laid out as follows: the top ground to your right, the second ground to your left, and the third in front of the hole. Then the bottom of the hole should be well dug up with the spade, leaving the last ground in the hole. The earlier the holes are thus finished before planting, the better; then, the longer the earth is exposed to the atmosphere, the more it will be fertilized. Before you begin to plant your vines, have the holes filled—for rooted vines to about six inches from the top, if for cuttings about ten inches.

[In regard to the distance between vines, we would observe that, for California, our opinion in regard to the space of eight feet has not changed; but we have some hesitation in expressing a recommendation for the same distance after having seen the fine Burgundy Pineau and the world-renowned Riesling planted so closely. Whether these grapes will give the same generous wine, with that exquisite bouquet, if planted eight feet apart,

K

remains to be proved by experiments. Our doubt originates from the generally established facts that, when vines are pruned for *quantity*, the *quality* will suffer. This fact is proved by scientific observation. The question which arises in our mind is, whether vines planted eight feet apart, producing eight pounds of grapes, pruned to the very minimum of the Californian yield, or whether sixteen vines, planted on eight feet of ground, producing one fourth of a pound of grapes to each vine, would make a better wine. It is true that one vine has, in the first case, as much soil to live on as sixteen vines in the other, but whether the sixteen vines do not possess more roots, leaves, and power to extract from the atmosphere more congenial elements for the development of that fine quality and bouquet they should have, is a question which we are not prepared at this time to answer. It is our intention to make experiments on this subject in future, and it would be well if other planters in different localities would do the same.]

The ground to your right, being the top ground, is thrown into the bottom of the hole, then that to your left. This done, you proceed to

Planting.—There are two ways of planting—one with cuttings, and the other with one-year-old vines. There is a good deal of difference of opinion among good and practical vine-planters. Some argue that if a cutting is properly planted at once on the spot of its destination, it will be more advanced in its third year, and, consequently, it will bear in that year more than the rooted vine, which is first set as a cutting in the nursery, and the next year transplanted on its destined spot. It is reasonable to suppose this to be the case; but it still leaves a doubt in the mind whether a large tract of land can be, or will be, as well worked as a small one. In a nursery, by good care, the cuttings can be rooted four times as strong as in a large field; besides, in the latter case, whether the vine has good roots or not, it is left where first planted; but when the rooted vines are taken out of the nursery for transplanting, the planter will select only those having faultless roots. But the greatest advantage of the nursery is, in my opinion, the fact that if a planter intends to plant one hundred acres of vineyard with cuttings, he will have to cultivate one hundred acres during the summer; but if he plants his cuttings for this one hundred acres in a nursery, two acres of ground will be enough to raise sixty-eight thousand rooted vines, the number required for one hundred acres. Now, to cultivate these two acres in the nursery, it will require ten days' labor with one horse;

while, on the contrary, for one hundred acres, during the months of March, April, May, June, and July (after that time no more plowing is required), you need two men and four horses—equal to two hundred and sixty days' work, and double that for the teams. Then the board of the men, and feed for the horses during that period. However, this is a matter of opinion, and each planter will follow his own idea, or will accommodate himself to surrounding circumstances. But now to the planting.

When the holes are filled as above described, if you plant cuttings, have them two feet long; bend the cuttings ten inches deep in the hole, near to a right angle, the lower part of which is laid horizontally on the bottom, and the upper part on the side wall of your hole, the top of it to be above the ground three inches. Then fill the hole from the ground surrounding the hole, which, of course, is top ground : then tramp the earth fast on your cutting, that no vacancy shall remain in the hole. Otherwise foul air will gather in said vacancy, and the cutting become mouldy, and will not live. But if you plant rooted vines, your holes will be filled to six inches. Now take your rooted vine, spread the roots on the bottom, and throw from the surrounding top ground on the roots ; shake it well, so that the pulverized ground shall get among the roots. Then tread gently with your foot round the root. It is still better if you prepare, from one part of fresh cow manure and three parts of black earth with water, a mud mixture of the consistency of tar. Put, before planting, your rooted vines in the same, and when so dipped, turn them in the bucket round and round. By this every root and fibre of the vines will be surrounded with this tar-like stuff, and prevent it from becoming mouldy under ground. After this, the ground in the front of the hole, taken out the last of the same, is to be leveled about the vine so as to leave a dish-like excavation around, as a receptacle and conductor of moisture to the roots. Be careful never to plant your vines too deep. It is better—if you make a mistake—to have them too shallow than too deep.

Cultivating.—The vines having been planted—either as cuttings or as rooted vines—in the month of January, the ground being recently plowed, not many weeds will be visible before the month of March. But this month it will be time to commence, either on account of weeds, or that the ground has already hardened around the vines, and requires stirring and pulverizing, so that the atmosphere may penetrate freely to the roots; for this pur-

pose the well-known shovel-plow is the best and most simple instrument, commonly used in the Western States to cultivate Indian corn. This requires one horse and a man. This plow can
go within an inch of the vines, and will consequently destroy all
weeds. First the plowman plows one way ; and then, when done
with the field thus, he plows crossways, by which operation any
weed escaping the first plowing will be destroyed without using
a hand-hoe. In this way, one man with two horses (one horse in
the forenoon and the other in the afternoon) will comfortably plow
three acres a day, on an average, in twenty-six working days of
the month. All plantations of vines one or more years old ought
to be plowed twice a month, as above described, to keep weeds
down, and stir up and pulverize the ground, by which means
you will charge it with nitrogen. This exposure of alternate
stratas of earth to the action of the sun, air, and rain, fertilizes the
soil incredibly. Moreover, the weeds plowed under ground by
their rotting enrich the soil, and impregnate it with ammonia and
humors. Then, a mellow ground is much more adapted to attract
moisture from the atmosphere than a hard-caked one.

Pruning, First Year.—When the last plowing at the end of July
is done, nothing more in the way of cultivation is necessary until
the end of December or beginning of January—the time for pruning. Your vines, if planted as cuttings, will have but small shoots ;
but if rooted vines, those shoots will be strong, and several of
them. In either case you cut the vine back to two eyes, being
always careful that all ground-shoots shall be clean cut away from
the main stem. Your pruning-knife must be sharp ; or, still better, use the grape-vine scissors, which are far superior to the knife,
and can be procured at the seed or hardware stores in San Francisco.

When the vine sprouts, which is about the month of March—
and sooner in this country—the planter must carefully inspect
his new vines, and break all sprouts out from the vine except
the two coming from the two eyes left for that purpose. This
done, the planter must again put his shovel-plow to work, and
cultivate the soil precisely in the same way as last year, described
above.

Pruning, Second Year.—Again, at the end of December, the
pruning begins, there having been two vines raised on each stem.
The one the most feeble or crushed is cut off; the other is left to
the length the planter wishes to raise his vine-stem.

[After several experiments, made on a large scale with vines pruned high and staked, and with vines pruned close to the ground, we have become convinced that low pruning close to the ground is the better mode in California; it gives better grapes, and ripens them a fortnight sooner. In consequence of these experiments, I left off, some years ago, high pruning and staking. My travels in Europe have proved to me the correctness of my experiments. There is but one view, that the closer you can keep the grapes to the ground the better they are. It would not do, however, to let the branches lie on the ground, as the summer rains would rot them; but in California and the south of Spain the grapes may and do lie on the ground, and on that account are sweeter.]

Pruning, Third Year.—The grapes having been gathered, the pruning will begin again in December or the beginning of January. This time there are three stems on the main stem. Two of these vines must be cut to two buds each, for making wood (for so-called water-branches or vines), to become the next year the bearing vines, and the third one of these vines cut to four buds, which will be quite sufficient to bear grapes; but if the main stem is quite thrifty, you may leave five buds.

[It has been before observed that where quantity is desired it is detrimental to the quality of the grape; therefore he who intends to make superior wine will do well to prune his vines to two buds instead of four and five. But if only ordinary table wine is desired for home consumption, the recommendation of five-bud pruning may be practiced.]

Pruning, Fourth and Subsequent Years.—Many and various are the opinions in pruning bearing vines. Some assert that the old way, to cut the vine back to from six to ten spurs, and on each spur to leave two or three buds, is the best; but on mature reflection, considering that the stem so cut has to make all the wood, besides to produce and ripen grapes, it is not reasonable to believe this mode to be correct, and, in fact, experiments in different countries and climates have proved this doctrine false. It is a well-established fact that the best mode of pruning is to cut the stem to three spurs each, with two buds, and leave three vines, each two or three feet long, according to the strength of your stem. The three spurs will grow this year wood for the next year's bearing, and the three long vines will grow the grapes. Next season the old three vines which have borne grapes this year are cut off to spurs with two buds each, and the three long vines originating from the last year's spurs are left to bear grapes this year, and so on alternately from year to year. This mode of pruning will insure a large crop every year, and will not exhaust the vine.

[The above paragraph will stand true in several wine-growing countries in Europe, especially on the Rhine and in some parts of Hungary; but in California, the vines pruned three or four feet long will bear so enormously that the wine will prove inferior; and if the vine bears the blue grape it will hardly become blue, but remains a pale pink, and will not give proper color to red wine.]

Summer Pruning.—The native Californians never used to prune vines in the summer, but let them grow any length they pleased. This is erroneous. Every person, on reflection, can at once see that the sap required to grow and produce vines ten, and often twenty feet long, may be better used if it is forced into the grapes. Undoubtedly the berries and bunches will be larger if moderately trimmed; besides, this trimming is a great advantage when the grapes are gathered, as the picking is so much easier than in an untrimmed vineyard, where every thing is tangled up. The best mode is to cut the tops of the vines to the height of five or six feet from the ground, in the month of July for the first time, and the second time in the middle of August. This operation is done easily, and pretty quick. One man with a sickle tops off about two thousand five hundred a day. Besides the above-named advantages, there is one more, viz., when the top is cut off, every where small vines will spring out and form a dense leaf on the ends of the vines, keeping the grapes growing underneath in a moderate shade, and making them thus more tender, juicy, and sweet. It is therefore a great mistake, practiced often by newcomers from modern Europe, that they will break out the so-called suckers; that is, little branches starting out behind the leaf, and growing feebly up to the length of a few inches. These, in the northern parts of Europe, are broken up, but not in Italy, Greece, Smyrna, etc. Now California having a warmer climate, the vines need more protection against the sun than elsewhere, and experience shows that where some bunches of grapes are exposed, without the shelter of their leaves, to the rays of the sun, the berries remain small, green, hard, and sour.

Crushing.—When the picked grapes are brought to the press-house, they ought to be crushed immediately, and not left standing in tubs overnight or the next day. The crusher is a simple machine. There are three cast iron cylinders; two of them, of even size, roll against each other; the third one is on top of the two lower ones, and is fluted, for the purpose of taking hold of the bunch and pressing it down to the two lower ones. These latter have very small projections, like a waffle-iron, so as to crush the grapes; but not the grape-seed, which would be injurious to the taste of the wine. I have one of these crushers, made to crush apples for cider, and it answers admirably. Two men crush easily with it five thousand pounds of grapes in a day.

[Opinions vary much in Europe with regard to crushing or stamping grapes with the feet. Our opinion is, that cylinder crushing is as good as treading, if it does not crack the seeds of the grape. Two wooden rollers, eighteen inches in diameter and two feet long, with a hopper on the top into which the grapes are poured, will crush grapes enough to make fifteen hundred gallons per day, with two men in attendance.]

Cost of Planting a Vineyard.—This, of course, will vary with the price of labor, locality, and soil; but to give an idea to persons who have no practical knowledge, I will give here a correct account of the planting of a vineyard of one hundred acres. This was actually expended on the same in labor and money, as I kept a strict account of every thing. The soil is red clay, intermixed with volcanic rocks, partly decayed and partly in the process of decaying. The land had been previously cultivated for grains. This hundred acres was planted in January, 1858.

FIRST YEAR.

Six men (with 9 horses for deep tiller, and 6 horses for shovel-plow), 20 days each, = 120 days, $35 per month wages, and $15 for board : =120 days, at $1 93...............................	$231 60	
Horse-hire 50 cents, feed 25 cents per day : 15 horses, 20 days each...	225 00	
Blacksmith's bill, wear and tear of harness..........................	30 00	
Eighteen men laying out, staking, and digging holes, 21 days each, = 378 days; and 6 men planting, 23 days each, = 138 days : wages $30, and board $15 per month, =516 days, at $1 73..	892 68	
Thirty-two days' work was spent in digging the rooted vines in the nursery; their cultivation during the summer brought their cost to one quarter of a cent each : 68,000 vines, at $2 50 per 1000	170 00	
Sundry expenses..	55 36	
Total cost of planting.....................................	$1604 64	
First summer's expense of cultivation, 260 days' work, with board, $50 per month.............................	$500 00	
Horse-hire and feed for 5 months.........................	205 00	
Blacksmith's bill, and wear and tear of harness.......	15 00	
Pruning, first year, in January...........................	25 00	745 00
Total first year's expenditure...........................		$2349 64

SECOND YEAR.

Replanting vines which died out from the year's planting and sprouting..	60 00	
Summer cultivation and fall pruning, as last year.................	745 00	
Second year's expenditure................................		$805 00

THIRD YEAR.

Sprouting and additional expenses for pruning, as this goes slower this year..	120 00	
Summer cultivation as above..	745 00	
Total third year's expenditure.........................		$865 00
Total expenses of 100 acres up to bearing....................		$4019 64

Here we may state that wine raised on my vineyard, of the vintages of different years, was taken by me to Europe to be tested by *connoisseurs* of wine, and for its quality and fitness to stand the ocean transportation. It was found by the best judges to stand the voyage well, and was pronounced eminently adapted for the manufacture of Champagne. On our return we visited Kohler & Co.'s California wine establishment in New York, and found their wines very good.

Many of our people are of the opinion that wine-producing may be overdone in California and in the Atlantic States. This fear is totally unfounded; as a proof of which, I will refer the reader to the valuable pamphlet of Mr. B. de Szemere, ex-minister of Hungary, and a resident of Paris since 1859. He gives the number of acres planted in France at 5,000,000, and the produce at 750,000,000 gallons of wine; in Hungary, 3,000,000 of acres planted, producing 360,000,000 gallons.

M. de Szemere classifies France as the first of the wine-producing countries of the world, and still it imports largely from foreign countries; and, furthermore, it is an undeniable fact that millions of gallons of wine are manufactured without the aid of a single grape.

The exact words of the author on this subject are as follows:

"But there are other, and, indeed, culpable methods of adulteration very injurious to health. The marvelous discoveries which are daily made in chemical science are continually and skillfully applied, not only to improve, but to adulterate the wines. In this manner do the Germans sweeten their wines; in this manner they saturate them with sulphur, with a view to neutralize their natural propensity to become acid, not only in casks, but even in bottles; in this manner they give them the artificial, but to connoisseurs disgusting flavor of Muscat. This trade of spurious wines is carried on in France on a still larger scale. All is false in the wines; the color, the strength, the flavor, the age—even the name under which they are sold. There are wines which do not contain a drop of grape-juice. Even science is impotent to distinguish the true from the false, so complete is the imitation. You may every day see advertised in the French newspapers the *Sève de Médoc*, of which a small flaçon, costing three francs, is declared sufficient to give flavor to 600 litres.

"Paris and Cette are the principal seats of this fraudulent adulteration. It is practiced in both places on the most colossal scale. Certainly one half of the Parisian population drink, under the name of wine, a mixture of which there is not one drop of grape-juice. The police are unable to prevent this adulteration; but the laws punish it with great severity. Every week do the newspapers publish judgments against wine-merchants and grocers, in execution of which their wines—twenty, thirty, eighty hogsheads at once—are poured into the gutters. But this dishonest art is now so perfect that even clever chemists can with difficulty distinguish the true wine from the false. Such was the case in a very recent trial. The chemist, after reporting every ingredient of which the wine was composed, observed that if one of them were in less quantity he would have been unable to distinguish it from the natural wine. The prosecuted wine-merchant, who was present, listened attentively to the chemist's report, and at last asked him which ingredient it was. The chemist very imprudently told him, and the accused immediately answered, "I am very much obliged, sir; and I don't regret now my forty hogsheads of wine which will be destroyed, because now I am certain of my business.

"The quantity of the French home consumption is exactly known. Taking, as an example, the year 1857 : France produced 35,410,000 hectolitres; she imported, besides, foreign wine, 626,000 hectolitres; total, 36,026,000 hectolitres. Of this quantity, in France was consumed: as wine, 17,142,000 hectolitres; as spirit, 2,453,000 hectolitres; as vinegar, 222,000 hectolitres; total of the French consumption, 19,817,000 hectolitres. We see that what is left for stock and exportation is not too much, and still less if we consider such years as 1854, 1855, 1856, in which the total production was only 10,000,000, 15,000,000, and 21,000,000 hectolitres, instead of 35,000,000, as it was in 1857. If, therefore, France itself, in 1857, consumed more than she can produce in some years, is it unreasonable to doubt whether she would always be able to export natural and unadulterated wines? In any case, can one believe that under such circumstances old French wines could be found any where but in private cellars?"

About Hungary and its wines he says:

"1. With the exception of six counties, the vine is cultivated in all Hungary (in France *eleven* departments have no vines, and twenty-five departments produce only common wines unfit for exportation). Every wine has its name, derived from a town, a county, a mountain, or a lake. Some large districts are celebrated for their wines; but even in small and less-known localities excellent wines are to be found, concealed like treasures which only wait to be discovered. The most renowned wines are:

LIQUEUR WINES.

White.		Red.	
Tokay.	Soprony.	Ménes.	Villàny.
Ruszt.	Szent Gyœrgy.	Eger.	Kàrloviez.

TABLE WINES,

Érmellék.	Ménes.	Szerednye.	Villany.
Bakator.	Eger.	Neszmély.	Visonta.
Somlyó.	Szegszard.	Kœbànya.	Kàrloviez.
Balaton.	Badacsony.	Borsod, etc.	Nógrád, etc.
Buda.	Magyaràt.		

"Numberless are the varieties of wines, for they vary in every respect: in color, from dark to pale red, from green to golden-yellow; in strength, they are light or strong; in taste, dry or sweet, with more or less flavor. It may be that one or another may not suit one's taste, but it is impossible that every body should not find among these different wines one agreeable to him. What is necessary is to try all, and afterward choose the most suitable.

"2. The Hungarian wines are generally stronger than the French or the Rhine wines. The reason of this may be sought in the kind of grape, in the properties of the soil, in the peculiar climate of the country, and finally, I think, in the fact that in Hungary the vineyards are commonly situated upon elevated hills, I dare even call them mountains. The Hungarians, knowing the old Latin proverb, *Bacchus colles amat* ("Bacchus loves the hills"), have followed the advice; they even now laugh at and despise the wines growing in the low plains, which is the case with most French wines.

"And this is not all. Two contrary tendencies are very perceptible in the two countries. The demand for French wines being great, the French cultivators, for thirty or forty years past, have left the finest wines out of account; they prefer the inferior sorts at a low price to the finer at a high price; they plant the vines close together, thus depriving the fruit of sun and air; they choose a rich soil, which gives a more abundant but an inferior produce; they, with the same object in view, make too much use of manure, which injures the quality of the wine (a practice once forbidden by *law*); in a word, the French wine has lost in flavor what it has gained in fecundity; quality has been sacrificed to the quantity.

"But in Hungary the contrary still prevails—that old system under which the quality is the principal object in view, under which a favorable exposure is the all-important consideration;

and the poor, light, stony, granitic land, from whence alone the choicest and the most highly-flavored wines can be obtained, is preferred to a rich, manured soil, insuring an abundant, but, in quality, far inferior return.

"Nothing is grander or more beautiful than our mountains, crowned either with shady woods or with vines of exuberant vegetation. Where you see a mountain, there you will find our vineyards. The superb *Badacsony* mountains form a high semicircle around the majestic Lake of Balaton, covering a surface of one hundred and twenty-five English square miles. The arid mountains of Ménes or Vilàgos overlook proudly the rich plains of Bà-nat, the holy Canaan of Hungary. The mountain called Tokay rises, in an another large plain, like a lofty pyramid. It has the form of Vesuvius, and, indeed, its existing but silent crater, its volcanic formation, shows evidently that it was once a fire-spreading mountain. The cultivation of such a soil is very difficult and expensive, the produce obtained but little; but then the latent fire of this volcanic mountain is what we call Tokay wine.

"Now I do not mean to say that the best wine is that which contains the most alcohol; this is only one of its elements; and other qualities, as delicacy, taste, flavor, are equally essential. My intention is to establish that, as the Hungarian *natural* wine is stronger than the Rhine, French, or even Spanish or Portuguese wines (taken without the usual addition of brandy), we may reasonably presume, first, that the Hungarian wine is particularly adapted to the English climate, and then that it will, more than any other light wine, facilitate to the English consumer the transition from the spirits and brandied wine to natural ones, which are undoubtedly more beneficial to the human health.

"It is a fact universally known, that to all wines exported to England is added more or less brandy (and in most cases not Cognac, but what is quite another thing, corn, fig, sugar-brandy); thus the Rhine wines receive an addition of 2–5, the French 4–7, the Spanish and Port wines 8–15 per cent. of alcohol.

"This practice is in Hungary quite unknown. Notwithstanding the mentioned addition of brandy, the Rhine wines never mark above 10–14 degrees (of Sykes), and the *best* clarets, like Château Lafitte, do not reach 18; whereas the quite pure and natural Hungarian wines, when examined by the Custom-house Test Office in London, gave the following results:

Buda, red table wine	21.1	Neszmély, white table wine	19.4
Eger	21.5	Balaton	20.6
Szegszard	22.8	Bakator	20.6
Ménes, 1842	23.	Tokay dry	23.6

"But I think there could be found inferior wines not surpassing eighteen degrees; consequently their introduction (at the shilling duty) would be very advantageous to the great mass of the English consumers.

"3. In the third place, I will say that if there be a country where *real old* wines (from 1811 to 1855) are to be found, it is Hungary. This important fact has its reason: *first*, from this circumstance, that Hungary, like England, is the land of large estates. There are landowners producing yearly from 1000 to 20,000 hogsheads of wine. Beautiful and enormous cellars, cut in rocky mountains, widely extend their ramifications, like labyrinths or catacombs, where the wines are ranged year after year. It is a kind of aristocratic and family glory to have a full and rich cellar. The grandchildren can drink the wine produced by their ancestors, and gratefully remember the past old times. Some of them would not sell their wines, even if they could do it; but that is not an easy matter in Hungary. Why? Because, and that is the *second* reason, the internal consumption with us is very small. In Hungary the ladies never drink any thing but water; the men of the higher classes are temperate from principle and habit; the lower classes from necessity and custom. Therefore, in proportion to the number of inhabitants, little wine, and scarcely any wine brandy, is consumed; so that, I dare say, Hungary, with France, the richest wine-growing country in the world, is at the same time the most temperate.

"Is not this fact an argument to show that the light and natural wines are the most efficacious and surest preservatives against the use of fiery, intoxicating brandies?"

The above extracts will satisfy the skeptic that where commerce exists and transportation is easy, there need be no fear of overdoing the business of vine-raising. California possesses the commercial advantages, as well as facility of communication, between producer and merchant. The merchant can send his wine to foreign markets after it is one year old without adding a drop of brandy, as our wine will, as I stated before, bear transportation, and even improve beyond expectation. The time so spent on the sea is not lost, for the wine gets older and better, and will, in consequence, meet a better sale.

We give below a table of the wine produced in Europe, the quantity reduced from morgens to acres. Our statistics were extracted from a work by Gustave Rawald. Also the price and yield per acre of wine calculated in dollars. These calculations were made by ourselves from the figures given in the above work.

THE AVERAGE WINE PRODUCTION OF EUROPE REDUCED TO AMERICAN ACRES AND GALLONS.

	Acres.	Gallons.	Gallons per Acre.
Austria and her Provinces.........	2,685,950	714,000,000*	$265\frac{5}{6}$
Greece and the Grecian Islands...	41,781	8,160,000	$195\frac{3}{10}$
Ionian Islands (for raisins, over 42,000,000 lbs.)†	35,812	1,224,000	$34\frac{1}{5}$
Italy.....................................	2,887,970	1,275,000,000	$441\frac{1}{2}$
Switzerland and Belgium..........	76,400	2,550,000	$33\frac{3}{8}$
France.................................	5,013,774	884,000,000	$176\frac{2}{7}$
Spain	955,004	144,500,000	$151\frac{7}{10}$
Portugal	238,751	25,500,000	$106\frac{8}{10}$
Total....................	11,935,442	3,054,934,000	$255\frac{95}{100}$

Germany.

	Acres.	Gallons.	Gallons per Acre.
Saxony.................................	5,945	340,000	$57\frac{1}{6}$
Prussia	53,719	7,225,000	$134\frac{1}{2}$
Bavaria	125,344	20,400,000	$162\frac{3}{4}$
Wirtemberg	65,656	10,200,000	$155\frac{1}{2}$
Baden	65,656	7,140,000	$108\frac{3}{4}$
Hesse..................................	23,875	4,250,000	178
Nassau	10,143	2,550,000	$237\frac{1}{3}$
Total.....................	350,338	52,105,000	$148\frac{72}{100}$

The aggregate number of acres under wine culture in Europe is 12,285,780. The total average yield per year in Europe is 3,107,039,000 gallons.

The wines of Germany would bring, at 25 cents per gallon........ $13,026,250
And those of the other countries, " " " 763,733,500

Together............................... $776,759,750

In Germany the average income per acre would be thus.................. $37 18¾
In the other countries, taken together, per acre would be thus.......... 63 98¾
But, taking each county or state separately, their wines would bring, upon the above average price of 25 cents per gallon, as follows:

European Countries.

	Total Amount.	Per Acre.
Austria and her Provinces......................	$178,500,000	$66 46
Greece and the Grecian Islands	2,040,000	48 82
Ionian Islands	306,000	8 54
Italy...	318,750,000	110 37
Switzerland and Belgium........................	637,500	8 34
France...	221,000,000	44 07
Spain	36,125,000	37 92
Portugal	6,375,000	26 70
Total...................	$763,733,500	

German States.

	Total Amount.	Per Acre.
Saxony..	$85,000	$11 79
Prussia..	1,806,250	33 62
Bavaria	5,100,000	40 68
Wirtemberg	2,550,000	38 83
Baden	1,785,000	27 18
Hesse..	1,062,500	44 50
Nassau	637,500	59 33
Total.................................	$13,026,250	

* Of these 714,000,000 gallons, Hungary produces some 450,000,000.
† Cephalonia exports annually 4,200,000 lbs. of raisins ; Thiaki, 350,000 lbs. ; Zante, 8,000,000 lbs.

We have taken a low estimate, according to present prices, but still it amounts to the enormous sum of $776,759,750. This amount the producer receives; so that it would be safe to calculate that the merchants receive from the consumers double this sum.

Italy shows the highest yield to the acre, and yet does not come up to the California yield within 100 per cent.

It is well known that California has within its boundaries at least 5,000,000 acres of land well adapted for the vine culture. This land, even though it yield no better than Italy, will still amount to $551,858,208 33. This large sum may astonish the most sanguine; nevertheless, in another generation California will produce this result.

Below we give an abstract of the Wine Chronicle of Germany, taken from the Records of the Agricultural Society in Wirtemberg. These Records, dating from the year 1246, are from that time up to 1420 very meagre and much interrupted, but from 1420 up to 1852 quite complete and correct. During those 432 years there were, as to quality of the wine,

Those eminently distinguished only	11
Very good years for a good wine	28
Pretty good ones　"　"	118
Middling quality wines	76
Inferior　"　"	199
Total	432

Concerning the productiveness, there have been

Years of ample yield	114
"　middle　"	18
"　poorer　"	99
"　failures, or yields not paying expenses	201
Total	432

This statement gives a clear view of the disadvantages under which the culture of the grape is to be carried on in such a northern locality as are most of the States of Germany. While we have in California no year of failure on record, or by the tradition of our oldest settlers, cold Germany has her vine crops killed or seriously injured, upon an average, three years out of four. This simple fact evinces the superior advantages of California for the production of grapes and wine.